FORMAC FIELD GU

NOVA SCOTIA

BIRDS

Written and illustrated by Jeffrey C. Domm

Formac Publishing Company Limited
Halifax, Nova Scotia

Formac Publishing Company Limited recognizes the support of the Province of Nova Scotia through the Department of Communities, Culture and Heritage. We are pleased to work in partnership with the Culture Division to develop and promote our culture resources for all Nova Scotians. We acknowledge the financial support of the Government of Canada through the Canada Book Fund for our publishing activities. Formac Publishing acknowledges the support of the Canada Council for the Arts which last year invested $20.1 million in writing and publishing throughout Canada.

Library and Archives Canada Cataloguing in Publication

Domm, Jeffrey C., 1958-
    Formac field guide to Nova Scotia birds / written and illustrated by Jeffrey C. Domm. -- 2nd ed.

(Formac field guide)
Includes index.
Previously published under title: The new Formac pocketguide
    to Nova Scotia birds.
Issued also in electronic format.
ISBN 978-1-4595-0049-5

    1. Birds--Nova Scotia--Identification. 2. Bird watching-- Nova Scotia--Guidebooks. I. Title. II. Title: Field guide to Nova Scotia birds. III. Series: Formac field guide

QL685.5.N6D65 2012   598.09716   C2011-908710-3

Cartography by Peggy McCalla

Formac Publishing Company Limited
5502 Atlantic Street
Halifax, Nova Scotia
Canada B3H 1G4
www.formac.ca

Printed and bound in Korea.

Contents

Contents

Introduction

Nova Scotia is an excellent place to enjoy birdwatching. Not only is the province a rich mosaic of forest, meadow, river, lake, marsh, beach and ocean, it also lies on the Atlantic flyway, the migration path for birds on their seasonal journeys between breeding and wintering grounds. In summer and fall, hundreds of species can be identified around the province, many of them in full mating plumage.

It can be difficult to identify wild birds correctly, especially if they are a great distance away and foliage or other obstacles are blocking your view. The full-colour illustrations in this book, along with the visual keys and the descriptions, will help you quickly compare essential features.

Each illustration has been drawn especially for this guide from photographs, live observation, scientific specimens and written descriptions. They represent typical specimens. When comparing a bird with the illustration, one has to bear in mind that plumage varies from individual to individual. Many birds change plumage seasonally and the colours change in different light conditions.

This book is divided into two sections: Seashore and Water Birds followed by Inland Birds. Within each section, the birds are arranged into groups such as gulls, raptors or warblers, and birds that are of similar type and size are in close proximity.

Of the hundreds of birds that either reside or pass through Nova Scotia, a selection of 200 familiar species was chosen for this book. In addition to the very common and widely spread birds, there are those that have limited habitat, but are of great interest to birdwatching enthusiasts. Birds that breed in Nova Scotia are identified by having an accurate illustration of their egg. The Nova Scotia Birding Hot Spots section (pages 8-16) will guide you to a number of suggested areas that experienced birdwatchers have identified as places of high interest to naturalists.

Before setting out on a birdwatching trip in Nova Scotia, be sure to dress warmly and watch the weather. Storms can move in quickly over the ocean, bringing high winds and cold temperatures, even in summer. These changes can affect the number of birds you see, as well as dampen your spirits, if you are not well prepared.

With the help of this guide you will find that birdwatching is both rewarding and full of surprises. As you begin to recognize many of the birds of eastern North America, you will appreciate their abundant variety.

How to use this guide

Birds don't stay in one place for very long, so it is important to learn a few simple rules to help you quickly identify them. You will often see a seashore or water bird either feeding or flying. If it is on the water, you can watch to see if it dives, skims the surface or tips its head under water, leaving its tail feathers pointing to the sky. If it is flying, you can observe the beating pattern of its wings — are they quick wingbeats, is it soaring, does it flap its wings and then glide?

Viewing inland birds is a bit different. Most often what you see is a bird that is feeding; perhaps it is hopping along the ground or flitting from branch to branch. Maybe it is perched in a tree, preparing to fly away.

The visual keys given in this guide focus on the primary identifiable features of each bird, and include colour, outline and size. Because seashore and water birds are more often seen in flight than inland birds, and have a wider variety of food-gathering methods, we have also included flying pattern and feeding style.

Secondary features for both kinds of birds include foot type, egg colour and size, and observation calendar.

When you are looking at a bird, first estimate the size, then take note of the shape of the wings, tail, head, bill or beak and feet. Note any particular marks — patches, streaks, stripes and speckles. Finally, observe its movements.

Legend for visual keys

1 **Size identification** — the rectangle represents the page of this book, and the silhouette of the bird represents its size against this page.

2 **Foot type** — Tridactyl

Anisodactyl   Zygodactyl

3 **Flight characteristics** —

Quick wingbeats

Slow steady wingbeats

Soaring

Wingbeats followed by gliding

Category of Bird

1

Size Identification

2

Foot Type

3

Flying

4 Feeding technique —

Stabs and prodding motion

Grazing and dabbling

Diving head first

Dives from water's surface

Tip up feeding

Skims water surface

Feeding

5 Egg — actual size and shape unless otherwise indicated.

Egg

6 Backyard feeder — there are three types of bird feeders to which small birds might be attracted.

7 Birdhouse nester — some species are happy to make their nest in a manmade house, which you might hang in your garden.

Backyard Feeder

8 Nesting location (for inland birds only)

▼ Hollow in ground

▼ Waterside plants

▼ Bushes and thickets

▼ Cavities of trees

▼ Deciduous trees

▼ Conifers and tall trees

▼ Tall, dead, decaying trees

▼ Banks along rivers and ponds

▼ Cliffs and / or rocky ledges

Birdhouse Nester

9 Observation calendar — the bar gives the initial for each of the twelve months of the year. The deeper colour indicates the best months for seeing the species, according to known migration patterns.

Nesting Location

Observation Calendar

J F M A M J J A S O N D

Nova Scotia Birding

Marine Drive

1 Conrad Beach

Located at the end of Conrad Road, twenty minutes east of Dartmouth via Route 207, the dunes and broad marsh provide an environment where a variety of small inland birds can be seen.

2 Fox Point

A wonderful area within easy reach of the city offering an opportunity to see Common Eider, Piping Plover, Great Blue Heron, ducks, scoters and many other shorebirds. Featuring beach hiking trails through meadows and seagrass, it, too, is located on Conrad Road.

Northumberland Strait

Wallace

Amherst

Oxford

Joggins

Springhill

Debert

Truro

Parrsboro

Cape Split

Minas Basin

Maitland

Canning

Grand Pré

Kentville

Bay of Fundy

North Mountain

South Mountain

New Ross

Halifax

Enfield

Annapolis Royal

Digby

Bridgewater

Kejimkujik National Park

Brier Island

Liverpool

Kejimkujik National Park Seaside Adjunct

Yarmouth

Shelburne

Cape Sable Island

Hot Spots

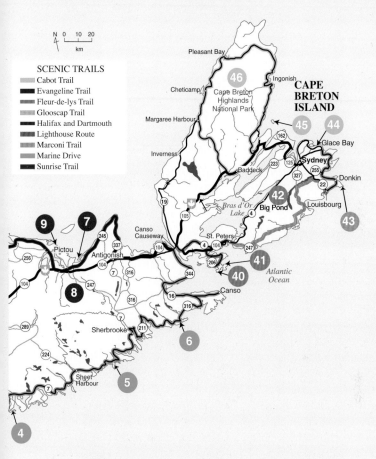

SCENIC TRAILS
- Cabot Trail
- Evangeline Trail
- Fleur-de-lys Trail
- Glooscap Trail
- Halifax and Dartmouth
- Lighthouse Route
- Marconi Trail
- Marine Drive
- Sunrise Trail

3 Three Fathom Harbour and Grand Desert

Three Fathom Harbour is just east of Lawrencetown Beach on Route 207. There are excellent viewing opportunities for flycatchers, warblers, sparrows and hawks around the marsh near Fishermen's Reserve. Grand Desert is located further along Route 207 on the Dyke Road. Park at the end and go right to find an old shooting range with dunes, or left to ascend a wooded hill and look out over the marshes. The hilltop offers an excellent view of the area and Bobolinks, nuthatches and Boreal Chickadees, as well as many other common species, can be seen.

4 Martinique Beach

Close to Musquodoboit Harbour, Martinique Beach is an exceptionally long stretch of marsh-dune-beach landscape. Around the marsh you can see hawks, warblers, finches and flycatchers, as well as the occasional bird of prey. The marsh is adjacent to a bird sanctuary where Canada Geese are known to appear in abundance during migration.

5 Taylors Head Provincial Park

East of Dartmouth on Route 7, Taylor Head Provincial Park is located near Spry Bay. This hiking area and beach offers birdwatching of many different kinds. The woods and fields are home to many inland species. Along the rocky shore, the beach and the sheltered parts of the shoreline one can see a variety of shore and sea birds.

6 Tor Bay Provincial Park

At one of the most easterly points of mainland Nova Scotia, Tor Bay features white sand beaches and rocky headlands. Many species of sea birds can be seen here, including some rare and transient birds. Located off Route 16 to Guysborough. Follow the signs to Larrys River.

Sunrise Trail

7 Merigomish Island

This long spit of land has a sheltered harbour on one side, the Northumberland Strait on the other. The feeding grounds at low tide are great places to see some rare birds, including the endangered Piping Plover. The best viewing is during spring and fall migration seasons. Exit 27 off Highway 104 toward Merigomish.

8 Melmerby Beach Provincial Park

Boardwalks provide a safe option for walking through the marshes and dunes. There are many species of shorebirds here, including plovers, yellowlegs, sandpipers, sanderlings and willet. Exit 25 or 27A off Highway 104 to Shore Road.

9 Caribou Provincial Park

This marsh and beach area is a favourite nesting and feeding ground for herons and ducks. There are opportunities for spotting rare and unusual species. Exit 22 (Highway 106) off Highway 104 to Pictou and follow signs to Route 6 and Caribou Island.

10 Wallace Bay Wildlife Area

The marsh at the head of Wallace Bay is preserved by Ducks Unlimited and the Canadian Wildlife Service. The trail, on a raised portion of a dyke, offers an opportunity to see many marsh birds, including Red-winged Blackbirds and many species of songbirds. Also in the Wallace area, at the mouth of the Wallace River, one can see Kingfishers, Northern Harriers, Kestrels and Bald Eagles.

11 Missaguash Marsh

The wetlands near the New Brunswick border are busy throughout the migration seasons. Thousands of birds move through the area, including herons, bitterns, rails, sandpipers, grebes and pintails, with some rare spotting opportunities. The dykes allow for easy hiking. Exit 1 off Highway 104 north of Amherst.

Glooscap Trail

12 Amherst Point Migratory Sanctuary

From spring to fall this area has an abundance of shore and sea birds, including northern shovelers, black terns, rails and bitterns. Marshes in the area offer excellent breeding grounds. Exit 3 at Amherst off Highway 104. Signs for the sanctuary are well posted.

13 Chignecto Game Sanctuary

A great place to spot grosbeaks, Gray Jays, White-winged Crossbills, Northern Goshawks, Pileated Woodpeckers and a variety of songbirds. Take Highway 2 out of Parrsboro for 12 km to the Boars Back Road.

14 Economy Mountain Trail

Located within Five Islands Provincial Park on Highway 2, this mixed-forest area is excellent for viewing Gray Jays, Northern Parula, Black-throated Green Warblers, Boreal Chickadees, Black-backed Woodpeckers and Ruffed Grouse.

15 Debert Game Sanctuary/ McElmon's Pond

This location offers some great birdwatching and a variety of habitats. Songbirds of many kinds nest here, including Cedar Waxwings, Eastern Wood-pewees, kinglets, vireos and warblers. With all this activity you are also bound to see a few hawks. Take Trans-Canada Highway to Debert (Exit 13) and watch for signs and a picnic park.

16 Victoria Park

A mixed-forest area, this park is home to many year-round inhabitants, including chickadees, jays, woodpeckers, kinglets, thrushes, warblers and several species of hawks and owls. Willow Street, in Truro.

17 Shubenacadie River

There are many sites along the Shubenacadie River where one can see Bald Eagles. Route 2 from Enfield and Route 215 from Shubenacadie follow the river quite closely. Alternatively, one can take a boat trip to see the nesting sites on the cliffs at the lower end of the river.

Evangeline Trail

18 Uniacke Estate Museum Park

This 2,125-hectare (5,000-acre) estate offers a range of walking trails in old-growth forests, meadows and around the lakeshore. A wide variety of warblers and other small songbirds, as well as hawks, can be seen here. On Highway 101, follow the signs for Mount Uniacke and the park.

19 Evangeline Beach

Although the majority of spottings that take place here are waterfowl, it is also possible to see birds of prey pursuing migrating birds. Best times for birdwatching are spring and fall.

20 Wolfville

At the Robie Tufts Nature Centre one can see Chimney Swifts gather throughout the summer, as well as find information about birding places in the Wolfville area. Merlins have been known to nest right in the town and you may see them chasing swallows.

21 Sheffield Mills

Several years ago a local farmer began feed the Bald Eagles that visited the area during the winter months and now Sheffield Mills is perhaps the best place in central and south Nova Scotia for seeing large birds of prey, winter or summer. There are nesting birds in the area, along with Red-tailed Hawks, Rough-legged Hawks, ravens and crows. Some of the best interaction between eagles and ravens can be observed here. Exit 11 to Canning off Highway 101. Signs with eagle symbols lead you to Sheffield Mills.

South and North Mountains
Several species of owl have been encouraged in this area by the construction of nesting boxes. If you are good at imitating their hoots, you may be rewarded with an answer. Northern Harriers and Red-tailed Hawks are also found in the region, nesting on the Canard and Grand Pré dykes. March and April are courting months in the South and North Mountains of the Annapolis Valley.

 Annapolis Royal Historic Gardens
In the centre of Annapolis Royal there is a beautiful public garden. With all the blossoms in summer, you are sure to see Ruby-throated Hummingbirds dart across your path, as well as many songbirds and other small birds. On the backside of the garden is a marsh, which attracts Red-winged Blackbirds and hawks.

 Brier Island
This is one of the prime areas for birding in Nova Scotia. Shorebird activity throughout the spring, summer and fall includes sandpipers, Short-billed Dowitcher, yellowlegs, Sanderling and plovers. Some interesting inland birds can also be observed here. Take Highway 217 along Digby Neck. This trip includes two ferry rides.

 Mavillette Beach
This provincial park includes salt marsh and beach areas where sandpipers, plovers, Willet, ducks, Great Blue Heron and many other shore and sea birds can be observed. Off Highway 101 north from Yarmouth to Mavillette.

 Chebogue Meadows
These marsh and beach areas are perfect for spotting a variety of shore and sea birds, including mergansers, ducks, Kingfishers, Osprey and many others. This is an especially good area for observing migrating birds in spring and fall. On Highway 101 north from Yarmouth.

Lighthouse Route

27 **Seal Island**
This is considered one of the best locations on the Atlantic coast for sea birds. A two-hour boat trip from Clarks Harbour will take you to the island. The Nova Scotia Bird Society organizes many such trips.

28 Cape Sable Island

Beautiful dunes and shoreline offer some very good birding, especially during migration seasons. There are opportunities here for spotting rare birds and transient visitors. Take exit 29 off Highway 103 at Barrington. The information centre in Clarks Harbour can direct you to specific locations and boat trips to Cape Sable.

29 Blanche Cove

The salt marshes, beaches and woodlands on this peninsula offer a spectacular variety of birding opportunities. The area is a gathering ground for many migrating birds, such as sea ducks. The hike to the end of the peninsula is easy and takes less than 30 minutes. Exit 28 to Clyde River off Highway 103.

30 Black Point

This area has a variety of habitats: woodland, swamp, meadow, coastal and riverbank. Shore and sea birds are abundant, including eiders, terns and ducks. East from Sable River (Exit 23) off Highway 103. Parking at Black Point Beach.

31 Little Port l'Hebert

Salt marshes, sand flats, cobblestone beaches and uninhabited islands offer excellent nesting grounds for various gulls, Common Eider, guillemots and cormorants. Exit 23 off Highway 103. Parking available.

32 Kejimkujik National Park

The woodland trails in Keji are some of the best in the province for birdwatching, featuring and hearing a wide variety of inland birds, including warblers, finches, flycatchers and woodpeckers. There are also larger birds — hawks, eagles, and Ospreys. The park is on Route 8, between Liverpool and Annapolis Royal.

33 Cherry Hill Beach

This South Shore beach, near Bridgewater, is an excellent location to see inland birds that enjoy marshland. There is a boardwalk around the marsh and a very beautiful beach.

Halifax Regional Municipality

34 Duncans Cove

There are popular hiking trails here along a rocky shore and many species of shorebirds make for great birdwatching. Located on Duncans Cove Road off Route 349, south of Halifax.

Long Lake Park Reserve
Once part of the Halifax watershed, this 6,000-acre park has many trails. With several lakes and a variety of habitats, many species of inland birds, including finches, warblers, thrushes and the occasional owl can be seen and heard here. Located on the St. Margaret's Bay Road, just before the turn-off to Peggys Cove.

 Hemlock Ravine
A few minutes from downtown Halifax, very near the shores of Bedford Basin, is the woodland park called Hemlock Ravine, once part of a large estate owned by Sir John Wentworth. The paths meander through mixed woodland, which is home to chickadees, nuthatches, juncos, warblers and Ruffed Grouse.

 McNabs Island
At the entrance to Halifax Harbour is a large island that makes for an excellent daytrip from the city. There are hiking trails leading to old forts and secluded beaches. The island is home to Ospreys, as well as a wide variety of warblers, finches and flycatchers.

 Trans-Canada Trail
Recycling old rail beds to create trails, this route travels across marshes, through wooded areas and close to sandy beaches in the Cole Harbour area. This area is a treat for birdwatchers. Parking off Bissett Road in Cole Harbour.

 Cole Harbour Preservation Area
A part of the Trans-Canada Trail, you can see gulls, terns, cormorants, Osprey and many other species in this sheltered saltwater area. Located on Bissett Road, off Route 207 to Cole Harbour. There are two parking lots.

Fleur-de-lys Trail

 Isle Madame
This island provides good birdwatching opportunities. The shoreline is a feeding ground for shorebirds, while the lakes and woods are home to a variety of inland species. Take Route 320 to the island, which can be reached by causeway from Highway 104 at Louisdale.

Point Michaud Provincial Park

Situated on the Atlantic Ocean, this park has a beautiful beach with sand dunes. A system of ponds nearby offers additional birdwatching opportunities. Located on Route 247, east from St. Peters.

 Big Pond

Route 4, between Sydney and St. Peters, runs along a lake, providing some spectacular views and the opportunity to see Bald Eagles. At Big Pond there are organized nature tours to see the breeding grounds.

Marconi Trail

 Cape Perce

East of Donkin, on the trail that leads to Port Morien, look for an unpaved road, just past Schooner Pond Cove. The track leads to an abandoned mine where you can park. On your right there is a marsh that is home to a wide variety of birds. In the other direction, there are woods and, finally, an open headland. This is one of the best places in Cape Breton to view birds in various habitats.

Cabot Trail

 Glace Bay Sanctuary

Ocean, salt marsh and beach habitats offer excellent opportunities to sight terns, Blue Heron, ducks, cormorants, gulls, Willet and many other species. Exit 28 off Highway 4, near Glace Bay. No signs are posted, so it is best to ask for directions on your arrival in the area.

 Bird Island

A boat is the only way to reach this spectacular birding location. This rocky island is a breeding ground for the Atlantic Puffin and many other sea birds. Boat tours leave from Big Bras d'Or. Take Exit 15 off Highway 105.

 Cape Breton Highlands National Park

Many hiking trails in the park provide excellent birdwatching. In the forests of the Lone Sheiling Trail you will see and hear many songbirds; in the barrens and evergreens of the Benjies Lake Trail, you may come across an owl in the evening, and in the day, warblers and Cedar Waxwings. The Lake of Islands Trail offers a little of everything, going deep into the highlands, through hardwoods, softwoods and finally out into the barrens. Information on the trails can be obtained at the entrance to the park.

Seashore and Water Birds

From the motionless silhouette of a Great Blue Heron to the scurrying of sandpipers along the beach, the coastal landscapes of Canada's eastern provinces provide great opportunities to see many species of shore and water birds, both residents and migrants. Gulls, cormorants and other diving birds can be found in the sheltered bays along the Atlantic coast. On offshore islands one can see Atlantic Puffins, while guillemots, kittiwakes and many species of gull nest on steep cliffs.

The Bay of Fundy's beaches and vast mudflats are favourite feeding grounds for many shorebirds, waders and ducks. On the Atlantic Ocean shores, there are sand beaches and adjacent marshes that abound with residents and migrants. One beach-nesting species, the Piping Plover, receives protection under the Piping Plover Guardian Program. Signs are posted to mark nesting locations, and volunteers watch over the nests at critical times and conduct public education sessions in an effort to preserve this endangered species from disturbance.

Bird migration is one of the wonders of nature. Every year, migrant birds, especially ducks and geese, travel thousands of miles between their breeding grounds in the far north and their winter homes in the south. On their way they must stop to feed and also to wait out inclement weather.

The 75 water and shore birds in this section are those you are most likely to see in one of these habitats. Along with each full-colour illustration, there are visual keys depicting seasonal range, the size of the bird, the type of foot, its flight pattern and its characteristic way of feeding. The egg is shown for birds that breed in the province.

Canada Goose
Branta canadensis

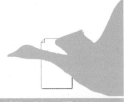

Size Identification

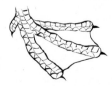

Foot: Tridactyl

Flying

Observation Calendar

J F M A M J J A S O N D

Male/Female: Black head, neck and bill; white cheek patch; breast and belly pale brown with white flecks; feet and legs black; back and wings brown with white edging; short black tail; white rump, seen in flight. *In flight*: Flies in "V" formations.

Feeding

Voice: Musical *honk*, repeated. Female slightly higher pitch *honk*.
Food: Grass, various seed, sand, grain.
Nest/Eggs: Large nest of twigs, moss and grass lined with down feathers placed near water's edge. 4-8 eggs.

Egg: 75%

18

Wood Duck

Aix sponsa

Size Identification

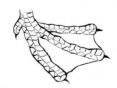

Foot: Tridactyl

Flying

Feeding

Observation Calendar

J F M A M J J A S O N D

Male: Green head and drooping crest; black cheeks; red eye and white throat with two spurs; bill orange with black markings; chest brown with white spots leading to white belly; black and green back; sides tan with white and black band. *In flight*: Long squared tail.

Female: Back and crown brown; white eye ring; speckled breast and lighter coloured belly.

Voice: Male — high-pitch whistle. Female — loud *oooooeeek* in flight.

Food: Aquatic plants, insects, minnows, amphibians.

Nest/Eggs: In cavity of tree, as high as 20 metres, or in a log or built structure lined with wood chips and feathers. 9-12 eggs.

Egg: Actual Size

American Wigeon

Anas americana

Foot: Tridactyl

Flying

Observation Calendar

J F M A M J J A S O N D

Feeding

Male: White patch running up forehead from bill; green around eye broadening at cheeks and descending on neck; brown changing to black on back and extremely pointed wings; pointed tail feathers are black, lines with white; bill white with black patches on top and on tip. *In flight*: Green on trailing edge of wing; white forewing and belly.

Female: Overall light brown with brighter colour running down sides. No green patch on eye.

Did you know? The American Wigeon is an opportunist: waiting for other diving ducks to come to the surface with their catch, they will attempt to steal the food.

Voice: Male — occasional distinctive whistle *wh-wh-whew*. Female quacks.

Food: Aquatic plants.

Nest/Eggs: Grasses lined with down, concealed under brush or tree, a distance from water. 9-12 eggs.

Egg: 90%

20

American Black Duck

Anas rubripes

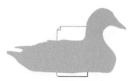

Size Identification

Foot: Tridactyl

Flying

Feeding

Observation Calendar

J F M A M J J A S O N D

Male: Dark black with hint of brown overall and blue speculum; bill is olive; feet and legs orange. *In flight*: White patches under wings.
Female: Overall lighter brown than male with orange and black bill.

Voice: Both female and male *quack*. Male also whistles.
Food: Vegetation, insects, amphibians, snails, seed, grain, berries.
Nest/Eggs: Depression on ground lined with grass, leaves and down, close to water's edge. 8-12 eggs

Egg: Actual Size

21

Mallard

Anas platyrhynchos

Observation Calendar

J F M A M J J A S O N D

Male: Bright green iridescent head, yellow bill; thin white collar; chestnut brown chest; grey sides; black and grey back; white tail; black curled feathers over rump; feet and legs orange. *In flight*: blue speculum with white border, underparts of wings grey and brown.

Female: Overall brown streaked with orange bill, black patches on bill; white tail feathers.

Voice: Male — call soft *raeb* repeated. Female — loud *quacks* repeated.

Food: Aquatic plants, grain, insects.

Nest/Eggs: Shallow cup built of grasses and aquatic plants lined with feathers on ground concealed near water. 8-10 eggs.

Blue-winged Teal

Anas discors

Size Identification

Foot: Tridactyl

Flying

Observation Calendar

J F M A M J J A S O N D

Male: Grey head with crescent shaped white patch running up face, bill black; chest and belly brown; back and wings dark brown with buff highlights; blue and green speculum; feet and legs yellow.
Female: Overall brown speckled with pale blue speculum.

Voice: Male has high pitched *peeeep*. Female — *quack* is soft high-pitch.
Food: Aquatic plants, seeds.
Nest/Eggs: Pile of grasses lined with down, close to waters edge, concealed. 9-12 eggs.

Feeding

Egg: Actual Size

23

Northern Shoveler

Anas clypeata

Observation Calendar

J F M A M J J A S O N D

Male: Grey speckled head and neck; yellow eye; wide black bill; sides rust; mottled brown back. *In flight*: Green speculum; light blue wing patch.
Female: Overall brown with orange bill.

Voice: Low *quack* or *cluck*.
Food: Aquatic plants, duckweed, insects.
Nest/Eggs: Made from grasses in hollow on ground lined with down feathers at a distance from water. 8-12 eggs.

Northern Pintail

Anas acuta

Size Identification

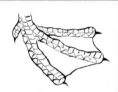

Foot: Tridactyl

Flying

Observation Calendar

J F M A M J J A S O N D

Male: Brown head with white line circling around cheeks to chest; white chest and belly; back and wings are black and grey; long tail is black and brown; rump black; sides grey with thin black banding; bill grey with white line. *In flight*: Long tail; white neck and line running up neck.

Female: Overall brown with black bill; no pintail feature.

Voice: Male has 2 high-pitched whistles. Female quacks.

Food: Aquatic plants, seeds, crustaceans, corn, grains.

Nest/Eggs: Bowl of sticks, twigs, grasses and lined with down at a distance from water's edge. 6-9 eggs.

Feeding

Egg: 90%

Green-winged Teal

Anas crecca

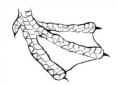

Observation Calendar
J F M A M J J A S O N D

Male: Head is rust with green patch running around eye to back of head, bill black, black at back of base of neck; warm grey body with thin black banding; distinctive white bar running down side just in front of wing; white rump; short square tail.
Female: Overall dull brown with green speculum; dark band running through eye.

Voice: Male — high pitched whistle. Female — weak shrill voice.
Food: Seeds, aquatic plants, corn, wheat, oats.
Nest/Eggs: On ground, cup shaped, filled with grasses and weeds, sometimes a distance from water. 10-12 eggs.

Ring-necked Duck

Aythya collaris

Observation Calendar

J F M A M J J A S O N D

Male: Back, head and breast black, high forehead; black bill with white outlines; yellow eyes; white spur on breast leading to grey underside and belly. *In flight*: Grey speculum; white belly.
Female: Grey cheeks and bill; one white band at tip of bill; white eye ring; dark charcoal back; brown chest, belly and sides.

Voice: Male has low, loud whistle. Female call is soft *prrrrrrrr* notes. Mostly quiet.
Food: Aquatic plants, molluscs, insects.
Nest/Eggs: Cup-shaped, built of grasses and moss and lined with down feathers, concealed near pond. 8-12 eggs.

Greater Scaup

Aythya marila

Size Identification

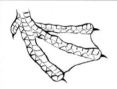

Foot: Tridactyl

Flying

Feeding

Observation Calendar

J F M A M J J A S O N D

Male: *Winter*: Dark green iridescent head neck and chest; white sides and belly; large flat grey bill; yellow eye; grey back with thin black banding; stubby black tail; black feet and legs. *Summer*: Sides and belly brown; head, neck and chest dull brown-black. *In flight*: Large white patches on inside of wings. **Female:** Overall dark brown with white face patch. Head held lower than male. *In flight*: Large white patches on trailing edge of wings.

Voice: Male — repeated *waaahooo*. Female — growling *arrrrr*. Mostly quiet.
Food: Aquatic plants, crustaceans, molluscs, snails.
Nest/Eggs: Cup-shaped clump of grasses and aquatic plants on ground, lined with down. Often builds on islands. 8-12 eggs.

Common Eider
Somateria mollissima

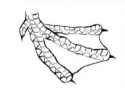

Foot: Tridactyl

Flying

Feeding

Observation Calendar

J F M A M J J A S O N D

Male: Large black patch on crown; white face; pale grey-green on back of head and from crown to beak. Overall white with black tail, belly and sides. *In flight*: Wing feathers black.
Female: Overall speckled brown with dark brown on head; bill grey; tail feathers often cocked.

Voice: Male *coooos* during courtship. Female — deep hoarse-sounding *quack*.
Food: Sea urchins, molluscs, crustaceans.
Nest/Eggs: Built of aquatic plants, moss and grasses lined with down feathers placed on ground, preferably rocky terrain. 3-5 eggs.

Egg: 90%

Harlequin Duck
Hiostrionicus histrionicus

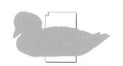

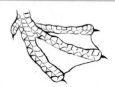

Foot: Tridactyl

Flying

Feeding

Male: Blue-grey head with white patch behind bill running up forehead; black bill; white ear patch. Black stripe on crown with chestnut brown on either side; white collar band and white patch on side of breast; chestnut brown sides; blue-grey back; black tail; feet and legs grey; small tail feathers. *In flight*: Long tail revealed; dark belly.
Female: Overall dark brown; white patches on face and behind eye; grey bill. *In flight*: White belly.

Voice: Male — high-pitched whistles. Female — agitated *ekekekek* and also *quacks*.
Food: Insects, molluscs.

Surf Scoter
Melanitta perspicillata

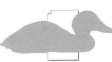

Observation Calendar

J F M A M J J A S O N D

Male: Overall black with white patches on forehead and back of neck; yellow eye; distinctive large orange and red bill with black and white patches on sides.
Female: Overall dark brown with large black bill and vertical white patch behind it; top of head is slightly darker. *In flight:* Pale grey belly.

Did you know? Easy spotting on the Surf Scoter is to look for birds diving directly into the breaking surf hunting for molluscs or crustaceans.

Voice: Male — low whistle during courtship.
Food: Mussels, crustaceans, insects, aquatic plants.

White-winged Scoter
Melanitta fusca

Size Identification

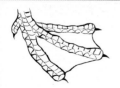

Foot: Tridactyl

Flying

Observation Calendar

J F M A M J J A S O N D

Feeding

Male: Black overall with yellow eye and white tear-shaped mark around eye; bill is orange, yellow and white; orange feet and legs. *In flight*: White wing patch.
Female: Brown overall; white oval on face; white patches on wings.

Voice: Female — low whistle. Male — in courtship is similar to ring of bell.
Food: Clams, scallops, mussels.

Black Scoter
Melanitta nigra

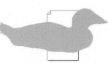
Size Identification

Foot: Tridactyl

Flying

Observation Calendar

J F M A M J J A S O N D

Male: Overall black with long thin tail feathers; large yellow knob on top of black bill; feet and legs dark orange.
Female: Overall dark grey with lighter grey on cheeks.

Voice: Low whistle during courtship. Quiet.
Food: Aquatic plants, molluscs, mussels, limpets.

Feeding

33

Long-tailed Duck

Clangula hyemalis

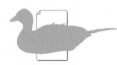

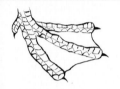

Observation Calendar

J F M A M J J A S O N D

Male: *Winter*: White head with grey cheek and black patch; bill black with tan band; white back with black and tan markings; black chest and white belly; very long tail feathers.
Female: *Winter*: White face, black crown; back brown with black wings; chest brown and white belly.

Voice: Male — call during courtship sounds similar to yodelling. Female — soft grunting and quacking.
Food: Insect larvae, molluscs, crustaceans.

Bufflehead

Bucephala albeola

Observation Calendar

J F M A M J J A S O N D

Male: Small compact duck; black head with large white patch behind the eye, grey bill; black back with white underparts.
Female: Grey-brown overall with smaller white patch behind the eye.

Voice: Mostly quiet. Male whistles. Female quacks.
Food: Small fish, crustaceans, molluscs and snails.

Common Goldeneye

Bucephala clangula

Observation Calendar

J F M A M J J A S O N D

Male: Black/green head with round white patch on cheek, close to black bill; back black with white bars; underside white; orange feet and legs. *In flight*: Large white speculum.
Female: Brown head and light charcoal overall; bill black with yellow patch; white patches on back. Both male and female are stocky with large head.

Voice: Call during courtship *jeeeeent*. Wings whistle when in flight. Female — low grating sound in flight.
Food: Molluscs, crustaceans, aquatic insects.
Nest/Eggs: In tree cavity or built structure lined with down. 8-12 eggs.

Hooded Merganser
Lophodytes cucullatus

Size Identification

Foot: Tridactyl

Flying

Feeding

Observation Calendar

J F M A M J J A S O N D

Male: Black crested head with large white patch on back of head behind eye; black bill is long and thin; rust eye; black back with rust sides and white underparts; black band runs down side into chest; white bands on black wings; tail is often cocked. *In flight*: Rapid energetic wing beats.
Female: Grey breast and belly; faint rust on back of crest; wings dark brown.

Voice: Call is low croaking or *gack*.
Food: Small fish, reptiles, crustaceans, molluscs, and aquatic insects.
Nest/Eggs: In tree cavity or built structure lined with grasses and down feathers, occasionally on ground. 9-12 eggs.

Egg: Actual Size

37

Common Merganser
Mergus merganser

Size Identification

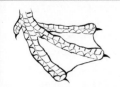

Foot: Tridactyl

Flying

Observation Calendar

J F M A M J J A S O N D

Male: Dark green head crested with red toothed bill slightly hooked at end; white ring around neck connects to white chest and belly; black back and white sides; feet and legs orange.
Female: Brown head and grey-brown back; white chin.

Feeding

Voice: Male call is *twaang*. Female call is series of hard notes.
Food: Small fish, crustaceans and molluscs.
Nest/Eggs: Built of reeds and grass and lined with down feathers in tree cavity, rock crevice, on ground or in built structure. 8-11 eggs.

Egg: Actual Size

Red-breasted Merganser

Mergus serrator

Observation Calendar

J F M A M J J A S O N D

Male: *Winter*: Dark green and black head with crest, red eye, white neck ring, long orange toothed bill with slight hook at end; chest white, spotted black; back black with white patching. *Summer*: Head chestnut brown; overall body grey. *In flight*: Rapid wing beats; straight flying pattern. Dark breast on male.
Female: Brown head with grey upper parts and white belly.

Voice: Call for male is *eoooow* usually during courtship. Female — series of hard notes. Mostly quiet.
Food: Small fish, molluscs, crustaceans.
Nest/Eggs: Built of grass and down in sheltered area under bush. 8-10 eggs.

Red-throated Loon

Gavia stellata

Size Identification

Foot: Tridactyl

Flying

Observation Calendar

J F M A M J J A S O N D

Feeding

Male/Female: *Winter*: Face changes from grey to white; red throat becomes white; grey speckled head; bill grey; white speckles on black back, white belly. *In flight*: Only loon capable of take off from land; quick wing beats over surface of water.

Voice: When breeding, a variety of high-pitched calls, but quieter than common loon.
Food: Small fish.

Common Loon

Gavia immer

Size Identification

Foot: Tridactyl

Flying

Feeding

Observation Calendar

J F M A M J J A S O N D

Male/Female: *Summer*: Black head and neck with white banded neck ring; thick grey sharp bill; red eye; white chest and belly; black back and wings spotted white; feet and legs black. *Winter*: Contrasting blacks and whites muted to dark dull brown. *In flight*: Large feet trail behind tail feathers; quick wing beats close to water's surface; takes off from water by running across surface.

Did you know? Loons can remain underwater for more than 5 minutes. They dive to feed and to avoid danger.

Voice: Drawn out *lou-lou-lou-lou* like yodelling, often at dusk or dawn.
Food: Small fish.
Nest/Eggs: Mound built with aquatic plants, mostly on islands. 2 eggs.

Egg: 75%

Pied-billed Grebe

Podilymbus podiceps

Observation Calendar

J F M A M J J A S O N D

Male/Female: *Summer*: Overall brown with grey-brown back; yellow eye ring; stout bill, white with distinct black band; black chin; short tail. *Winter*: White ring on bill softens; lighter chin. White tail feathers occasionally revealed when threatened by another bird. *In flight*: white patch on belly and white trail edge on wings.

Voice: Call is *cow* repeated with *keeech* at end, also various cluckings.
Food: Small fish, amphibians, crayfish, aquatic insects.
Nest/Eggs: Platform built with aquatic plants in shallow water attached to reeds and other aquatic plants. 5-7 eggs.

Red-necked Grebe

Podiceps grisegena

Size Identification

Foot: Tridactyl

Flying

Feeding

Observation Calendar

J F M A M J J A S O N D

Male/Female: *Summer*: Black crown with white cheeks and chin; long thick neck is rust blending to black back and wings; bill is broad yellow and black. *Winter*: Loses all colour except black and grey; bill remains yellow. *In flight*: white under-wings and belly, and white edges on wings.

Voice: Chattering, squeaks and long notes on breeding grounds. Quiet in winter.

Food: Small fish, aquatic insects, marine worms, molluscs, crustaceans.

American Coot

Fulica americana

Observation Calendar
J F M A M J J A S O N D

Male/Female: Duck-like body, slate-coloured overall; white bill and frontal shield shows red swelling at close range; partial black ring around tip of beak; feet and legs greenish-yellow; lobed toes.

Did you know? The American Coot has many different courtship displays, including running over the surface of water with its neck and head bent very low.

Voice: Variety of calls including clucks, grunts and other harsh notes and toots sounding like a small trumpet.
Food: Seeds, leaves, roots and small aquatic plants.
Nest/Eggs: Floating platform nest of dead leaves and stems lined with finer material and anchored to reeds. 8-10 eggs.

Common Black-headed Gull

Larus ridibundus

Foot: Tridactyl

Flying

Feeding

Observation Calendar

J F M A M J J A S O N D

Male/Female: *Summer*: Brown head that may appear black in early spring; white eye ring; thin red bill; neck chest and belly white; back and wings soft grey with black wing tips; white rump; black tail; feet and legs red. *In flight*: Tips of white wings blend to charcoal outlined in white.

Voice: Call is high-pitched harsh *uuup* and various squeals.
Food: Insects, earthworms and small fish.

Bonaparte's Gull

Larus philadelphia

Observation Calendar

J F M A M J J A S O N D

Male/Female: *Summer*: Smaller gull with dark head and bill; white neck, chest and belly; grey back and black tail feathers. *Winter*: During winter months black cap disappears and a small black spot on side of head turns white. *In flight*: wings appear black tipped.

Voice: Low rasping *gerrrr* or *wreeeek*.
Food: Small fish, worms and ground insects.
Nest/Eggs: Built of sticks and twigs and lined with grasses placed in spruce or fir tree 5-20 feet above ground. 3 eggs.

Ring-billed Gull

Larus delawarensis

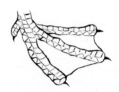

Observation Calendar

J F M A M J J A S O N D

Male/Female: *Summer*: White overall; yellow bill with black band at end; yellow eye; pale grey wings and black tips and white patches within black tips; black feet and legs. *Winter*: Feet and legs turn yellow; light brown spots on top of head and back of neck. *In flight*: grey underparts; black wing tips.

Voice: Loud *kaawk* and other calls.
Food: Insects, bird eggs, worms, garbage.
Nest/Eggs: Colonies. Grasses, sticks, twigs and pebbles built on ground. 3 eggs.

Herring Gull
Larus argentatus

Size Identification

Foot: Tridactyl

Flying

Feeding

Observation Calendar

J F M A M J J A S O N D

Male/Female: White head that in winter is streaked light brown; yellow eye and bill; small red patch on lower bill; tail black; feet and legs red. *In flight*: Grey wing with white on trailing edge and black tips; pale brown rump; wide charcoal tail feathers.

Voice: Variety of squawks and squeals. Aggressive alarm call is *kak kak kak kak* ending in *yucca*.
Food: Insects, small mammals, clams, fish, small birds, crustaceans, mussels, rodents, garbage.
Nest/Eggs: Colonies. Mound lined with grass and seaweed on ground or cliff. Usually on islands. 2-4 eggs.

Egg: 90%

Iceland Gull

Larus glaucoides kumlieni

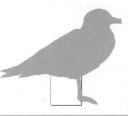

Observation Calendar

J F M A M J J A S O N D

Male/Female: Overall white with light grey back and wings; white wings underside; yellow bill with red tip on lower part; yellow eye; dark pink feet and legs. *In flight*: Overall white and grey underparts; white patches on wing tips.

Voice: Mostly quiet. Variety of squeaks.
Food: Fish, carrion, bird eggs.

Lesser Black-backed Gull

Larus fuscus

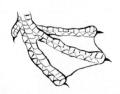

Observation Calendar

J F M A M J J A S O N D

Male/Female: Mostly white head with light brown streaking, yellow eye; yellow bill with small red patch; dark grey back and wings; black wing tips; feet and legs yellow. *In flight*: pale grey underparts; white on trailing edge of wing; black wing tip with small white spot.

Voice: Low pitched squawks and squeals.
Food: Insects, small birds, small mammals. Notable for stealing food from other gulls.

Glaucous Gull

Larus hyperboreus

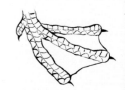

Observation Calendar

J F M A M J J A S O N D

Male/Female: Overall white with light grey back and wings; bill is yellow with red patch on lower portion at tip; yellow eye; pink legs and feet; short square white tail. *In flight*: White wing tips on grey wings.

Voice: Variety of squawks and other calls that are deep and hoarse sounding.

Food: Small mammals, birds, eggs, insects, garbage, small fish, crustaceans, carrion, molluscs.

Great Black-backed Gull

Larus marinus

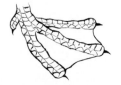

Foot: Tridactyl

Flying

Feeding

Egg:80%

Observation Calendar

J F M A M J J A S O N D

Male/Female: White head, chin, chest and belly, red patch on lower portion of bill; feet and legs pink/grey; black wings with thin white band on trailing edge; tail and back black.
In flight: Pale grey undersides with black wing tip; tail white.

Voice: Loud squawks and deep guttural notes.
Food: Scavenger. Small fish, mammals, young birds and garbage. Major predator of other birds including puffin and tern chicks.
Nest/Eggs: Colonies. Mound of seaweed and other coastal plants lined with grasses on ground or rocky ledge. 3 eggs.

Black-legged Kittiwake

Rissa tricactyla

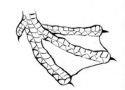

Observation Calendar

J F M A M J J A S O N D

Male/Female: White head, chest, belly and tail; bill yellow; wings grey with black triangular tips; feet and legs black. *Winter*: Dark grey patch behind eye. *In flight*: All grey upperparts of wings with black tips. Immature birds have large black patch on upper wings forming an "M" shape in flight.

Voice: Repetitive *kee* and *ketiwake*. Variety of notes.
Food: Small fish off surface of water.
Nest/Eggs: Colonies. Cup-shaped mud, seaweed and grass on rocky ledge or building. 2 eggs.

Common Tern
Sterna hirundo

Size Identification

Size Identification

Foot: Tridactyl

Flying

Feeding

Observation Calendar

J F M A M J J A S O N D

Male/Female: *Summer*: Soft grey overall with black-cap; white cheeks; long thin red bill with black tip; short, red feet and legs; wings and tail feathers grey, exceptionally long; white underside to tail. *Winter*: Black cap receeds leaving white face; black bar on wing; charcoal on tail. *In flight*: Charcoal on wing tips; grey overall; quick wingbeats.

Voice: Short *kip* repeated and louder *keeeear*.
Food: Small fish.
Nest/Eggs: Colonies. On ground, cup of grasses on sandy or pebbled areas. Most often on islands. 2-3 eggs.

Egg: Actual Size

Arctic Tern
Sterna paradisaea

Foot: Tridactyl

Flying

J F M A M J J A S O N D

Male/Female: Black head with long sharp red bill; overall grey; exceptionally long thin tail; red feet and legs are very short; *In flight*: White rump and lower back.

Did you know? Terns have the ability to hover over the surface of the water when hunting for prey.

Voice: Loud high-pitched *kee ar* or *kip-kip-kip-kee-ar*.
Food: Small fish.
Nest/Eggs: On ground, lined with grasses and shells, on rocky ledge or beach, often in colonies, isolated from human habitation. 2 eggs.

Feeding

Egg: Actual Size

55

Black Tern

Childonias niger

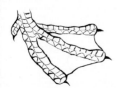

Observation Calendar

J F M A M J J A S O N D

Male/Female: *Summer*: Black head, bill, chest and belly; white rump; feet and legs black; wings and tail charcoal. *Winter*: Wings and back charcoal; head white with black on top; white chest and underparts.

Did you know? This is one very fast bird. The Black Tern catches insects in flight.

Voice: Call is short *kirc* of *keeeel*.
Food: Insects.
Nest: Colonies. Loosely built pile of aquatic plants and grasses on water's edge or floating on water. 3 eggs.

Northern Gannet

Morus bassanus

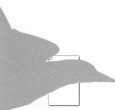

Size Identification

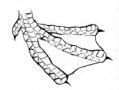

Foot: Tridactyl

Flying

Observation Calendar

J F M A M J J A S O N D

Male/Female: Overall white with black wing tips; pale yellow on side of head; broad grey bill; yellow eye surrounded by black eye ring.

Did you know? When Northern Gannets dive, they fold their wings, becoming like arrowheads. When you see Northern Gannets feeding it is a clue that whales may also be in the area chasing schools of fish.

Feeding

Voice: Low croaks and grunts, during courtship.
Food: Schooling fish including mackerel and herring.

Egg: 80%

Double-crested Cormorant

Phalacrocorax auritus

Observation Calendar

J F M A M J J A S O N D

Male/Female: Overall black with long tail feathers; bright orange chin and throat patch, feet and legs black. Crest is visible only during courtship. *In flight*: Neck is kinked.

Did you know? Cormorants are often seen perched on a rock or pier with wings fully extended to dry their feathers.

Often seen flying extremely high.

Voice: Call is a variety of grunts and croaks, only at its nest. Elsewhere silent.
Food: Small fish.
Nest/Eggs: Colonies. Platform built of sticks and twigs lined with leaves, grass and placed on ground or small tree. 3-5 eggs.

Great Cormorant

Phalacrocorax carbo

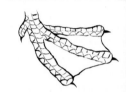

Observation Calendar

J F M A M J J A S O N D

Male/Female: Overall black with large grey bill hooked at end; yellow where bill meets the throat, white cheeks and throat; black feet and legs. Larger than Double-crested Cormorant.

Did you know? Cormorants will fly in V-formations in small flocks and are silent in flight.

Voice: Variety of grunt-like calls and a croak only at its nest. Elsewhere silent.
Food: Many different types of fish.
Nest/Eggs: Colonies. Platform of sticks lined with seaweed on rocky ledge near water or isolated on an island. 3-4 eggs.

Dovekie
Alle alle

Size Identification

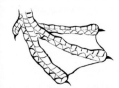

Foot: Tridactyl

Flying

Observation Calendar
J F M A M J J A S O N D

Feeding

Male/Female: Small black head and back, short stout black bill, small white line above eye; white belly; feet and legs black; short black tail. *Winter*: Chin and throat turn white.
In flight: Very quick wing beats that are often blurred.

Spends most of its time on the open ocean.

Voice: Variety of chattering and squeaking notes.
Food: Crustaceans, plankton.

Common Murre

Uria aalge

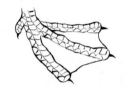

Foot: Tridactyl

Flying

Feeding

Observation Calendar

J F M A M J J A S O N D

Male/Female: *Summer:* Black overall with white chest and belly; long black bill; feet and legs black. *Winter:* White throat and cheeks; dark line through cheek. *In flight:* White underparts.

Did you know? The Murre is capable of diving down to depths of 100 metres or more.

Voice: Purr-like low *muurrrr* sounds similar to its name, also growls.
Food: Small fish.
Nest/Eggs: Colonies. No nest material except a few pebbles on a rocky ledge. Egg colours and patterns will vary. 1 egg.

Egg: 75%

Thick-billed Murre

Uria lomvia

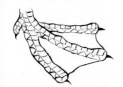

Observation Calendar

J F M A M J J A S O N D

Male/Female: *Summer*: Black overall with white chest and belly; distinctive white line runs along edge of sharp bill; thin white bands on wings; feet and legs black. *Winter*: Dark greyish over-all with white chin, cheeks, chest and belly. *In flight*: White belly.

Voice: Purr-like low *muurrrr* sounds similar to its name, also growls.
Food: Small fish.

Razorbill
Alca torda

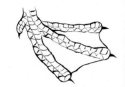

Foot: Tridactyl

Flying

Feeding

Observation Calendar
J F M A M J J A S O N D

Male/Female: Black head, neck and back with white line running under eye to top of bill; bill black with white and grey lines running down to tip; chest and belly white; feet and legs black; black wings and pointed tail feathers are often cocked; thick neck.

Did you know? The Razorbill can dive down 100 metres and stay under water for almost a minute.

Voice: Various croak-like sounds and growls.
Food: Small fish.
Nest/Eggs: Colonies. Twigs placed on rocky ledge or in burrow between boulders, but sometimes no nest built. 1 egg.

Egg: 90%

Black Guillemot

Cepphus grylle

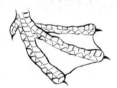

Observation Calendar
J F M A M J J A S O N D

Male/Female: Black overall with white oval patch on wing; feet and legs orange; bill is black with bright red inside mouth. *Winter*: White head, chest and belly. *In flight*: White under wings.

Voice: High pitched *squeaks*.
Food: Fish and crustaceans.
Nest/Eggs: On ground and in cracks on cliffs, concealed by drift-wood, sticks and boulders. 1-2 eggs.

Atlantic Puffin

Fratercula artica

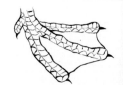

Observation Calendar

J F M A M J J A S O N D

Male/Female: *Summer:* Only puffin in eastern regions. Large colourful bill with white mask; black collar, head and back; white chest and belly; orange eye ring; wings and tail black; orange feet and legs. *Winter:* Markings slightly duller.

Voice: Hard sounding *urrrr* and croaks.
Food: Small fish, crustaceans and squid.
Nest/Eggs: Colonies. A rock crevice under boulder lined with grasses or a burrow dug in soft sand. 1 egg.

American Bittern

Botaurus lentiginosus

Observation Calendar

J F M A M J J A S O N D

Male/Female: Overall reddish brown with white stripes on underside; yellow bill long and sharp; short brown tail lightly banded; smudgy brown back. *In flight*: Tips of wings dark brown.

Did you know? The American Bittern is extremely difficult to spot in the field because, if approached, it will freeze and blend into the reeds.

Voice: *In flight*, a loud *squark*. Song is a loud *kong-chu-chunk*, on breeding grounds.
Food: Small fish, reptiles, amphibians, insects, small mammals.
Nest/Eggs: Concealed platform built from aquatic plants just above water. 2-6 eggs.

Great Blue Heron

Ardea herodias

Foot: Anisodactyl

Flying

Feeding

Observation Calendar

J F M A M J J A S O N D

Male/Female: Overall grey-blue with black crest on top of head; long neck and bill; black patch connecting eye and long yellow bill; white head; long grey legs and feet; long feathers extend over wings and base of neck. *In flight*: Neck is kinked; legs extend past tail; constant wing flapping with occasional glide.

Voice: Bill makes clacking sound. Call is harsh *squawk*.
Food: Small fish, reptiles, amphibians, crustaceans, birds, aquatic insects.
Nest/Eggs: Colonies. Platform of aquatic plants and twigs lined with softer materials such as down and soft grass, placed in tree or shrub. 3-7 eggs.

Egg: Actual Size

Black-bellied Plover
Pluvialis squatarola

Observation Calendar

J F M A M J J A S O N D

Male/Female: *Summer*: Black mask set against pale grey speckled head, crown and neck; bill black; breast and belly black; wings and tail black with white speckles; white rump; feet and legs black. *Winter*: Black face patch; dull grey-brown chest and belly. *In flight*: Black on inner wings underparts; white wing band; white rump.

Voice: Call is whistled 3-note *pee oo ee*.
Food: Marine worms, insects, crustaceans, molluscs, seeds.

American Golden-Plover

Pluvialis dominica

Observation Calendar

J F M A M J J A S O N D

Male/Female: *Summer*: Crown, back of neck, back and wings black or dark grey strongly speckled with yellow; black face mask running into breast and black belly and rump; white runs from forehead down side of neck to chest; grey legs.
Winter: Strong contrasting colours change to soft grey on face, head, chest and belly. Yellow speckles are muted.
In flight: Dark underwings; grey patch on inner wing near body.

Voice: Call is soft *kuee-leee*.
Food: Molluscs, aquatic insects, marine worms.

Semipalmated Plover
Charadrius semipalmatus

Size Identification

Foot: Anisodactyl

Flying

Feeding

Observation Calendar

J F M A M J J A S O N D

Male/Female: *Summer*: Dark brown head, back and wings; small white patch on forehead with black band above; faint white eyebrow; white chin extending into white collar with black collar band below; chest and belly white; wing feathers black; feet and legs orange; bill is orange tipped in black.
In flight: Quick wingbeats with slight glide just before landing.

Voice: Whistle *chee-weee* with a defensive call in quick short notes. Also soft rattling.
Food: Marine worms.
Nest/Eggs: Hollow on ground with shell bits and grass on sand or gravel. 4 eggs.

Egg: Actual Size

Piping Plover
Charadrius melodus

Foot: Anisodactyl

Flying

Feeding

Observation Calendar

J F M A M J J A S O N D

Male/Female: *Spring and Summer*: Light greyish upperparts with distinctive black band across forehead; bill yellow with black tip; black collar; white chin, cheeks, chest and belly; black wing feathers; feet and legs yellow.
Winter: Black collar band becomes grey; bill black.
In flight: Quick wingbeats with slight glide just before landing; white at base of tail and black tail feathers.

Did you know? The Piping Plover is an endangered species and its nesting grounds are under special protection.

Voice: Call is soft whistled *peeeep*.
Food: Insect larvae, molluscs, crustaceans, fly larvae and marine worms.
Nest/Eggs: Scraped out hollow on sand with a few pebbles or shells. 3-4 eggs.

Egg: Actual Size

Greater Yellowlegs
Tringa melanoleuca

Size Identification

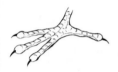

Foot: Anisodactyl

Flying

Observation Calendar

J F M A M J J A S O N D

Male/Female: Speckled grey and white overall; long bright yellow legs and feet; long straight black bill; short tail feathers with black banding; white belly.

Feeding

Voice: Call is whistled musical *whew* repeated and descending.
Food: Fish, snails, insects, plants.
Nest/Eggs: Hollow on ground in damp area. 4 eggs.

Egg: Actual Size

Lesser Yellowlegs
Tringa flavipes

Size Identification

Foot: Anisodactyl

Flying

Feeding

Observation Calendar
J F M A M J J A S O N D

Male/Female: Long black bill; dark upperparts speckled white; white belly; wings and tail feathers banded black; long yellow legs and feet.

Voice: Call is *tu* repeated.
Food: Insects, worms, snails, berries, small fish.

Willet

Catoptrophorus semipalmatus

Observation Calendar

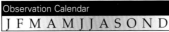

J F M A M J J A S O N D

Male/Female: Brownish grey and white speckled; white at lower belly and rump; bill is long, heavy greyish yellow; feet and legs grey; black tip on wings.
In flight: Distinctive bold white wing band on black tipped wings.

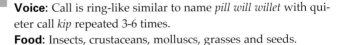

Voice: Call is ring-like similar to name *pill will willet* with quieter call *kip* repeated 3-6 times.
Food: Insects, crustaceans, molluscs, grasses and seeds.
Nest/Eggs: On open ground, lined with grasses or bits of shell, a distance from water. 4 eggs.

Spotted Sandpiper

Actitis macularia

Observation Calendar
J F M A M J J A S O N D

Male/Female: *Summer*: Grey-brown on head, back and wings; white eyebrow and black line running from beak to back of neck; long orange bill; white chin, chest and belly with distinct charcoal spots; yellow feet and legs; bobbing tail.
Winter: White underparts — no spots. *In flight*: Quick stiff wingbeats, slightly arched back.

Voice: Quiet bird but makes a *peeetaawet* call during courtship and a whistle that is repeated when alarmed.
Food: Insects, worms, crustaceans, fish, flies and beetles.
Nest/Eggs: Shallow depression on ground lined with grasses and mosses. 4 eggs.

Whimbrel

Numenius phaeopus

Foot: Anisodactyl

Flying

Observation Calendar

J F M A M J J A S O N D

Feeding

Male/Female: Overall grey and brown speckled with cream sides banded with dark brown; long downward curving black bill with yellow underside; cream eyebrow extending from bill; dark brown cap; feet and legs grey; tail brown with dark brown banding.

Voice: Inflight call is rapid *qui* repeated numerous times with no change in pitch.

Food: Insects, marine worms, crustaceans, mollusks, crabs, berries.

Nest/Eggs: Depression lined with lichens or sedge leaves. 4 eggs.

Egg: 90%

Ruddy Turnstone
Arenaria interpres

Observation Calendar
J F M A M J J A S O N D

Male/Female: *Winter*: Speckled brown back, head and wings; white belly, brown bib and white patch on either side; feet and legs dark orange. *Summer*: Overall upperparts brown and black; brown and black bill with white patch just behind bill; black bib with white patch; short black tail. *In flight*: White bands on wings and back.

Did you know? The Ruddy Turnstone got its name because of its feeding habits. The bird wanders down the feeding area turning over stones.

Voice: Call is *tuc e tuc*.
Food: Insects, molluscs, crustaceans, marine worms.

Red Knot
Calidris canutus

Size Identification

Foot: Anisodactyl

Flying

Observation Calendar

J F M A M J J A S O N D

Feeding

Male/Female: *Winter:* Face, neck and chest turn from brick red in summer to light grey; wings and tail turn dark; black bill; legs and feet charcoal.

Did you know? Red Knots are mostly seen flying in flocks of hundreds of birds with Dunlins, plovers, Godwits, sandpipers and many other shorebirds in their migration south or north.

Voice: Call is low *nuuuut*. Soft *currret* in flight.
Food: Molluscs, worms, insects, crabs, seeds.

Sanderling
Calidris alba

Observation Calendar
J F M A M J J A S O N D

Male/Female: *Summer*: Bright brown and speckled on head, back and breast; black tail; white belly; long bill is dark brown; feet and legs black. *Winter*: Light grey head, neck and chest; white cheeks, white belly; tail black. *In flight*: White on under-wing; white bar on top side of wing.

Voice: Call is *kip* in flight. Chattering during feeding.
Food: Crustaceans, molluscs, marine worms, insects.

Semipalmated Sandpiper

Calidris pusillus

Observation Calendar

J F M A M J J A S O N D

Male/Female: Short, straight black bill; back is grey-brown; white underparts; black legs with slightly webbed front toes. In winter, uniformly grey on back. *In flight*: distinctive formations of thousands of birds stretching hundreds of metres, showing white underparts in unison.

Voice: Continuous quavering *churrrk*.
Food: Small marine invertebrates usually on mud flats.
Nest/Eggs: Depression lined with grass and leaves on margins of fresh and salt water. 4 eggs.

Least Sandpiper
Calidris minutilla

Size Identification

Foot: Anisodactyl

Flying

Feeding

Observation Calendar

J F M A M J J A S O N D

Male/Female: Long downward curved black bill; overall brown and black; belly and rump white; feet and legs are yellow. Overall colour turns grey in non-breeding seasons. *In flight*: V-shaped wings white on undersides.

Voice: High pitched *kreeeep* rising up. When in flock it gives high repeated notes.
Food: Insects, mollusks, crustaceans and marine worms.
Nest/Eggs: Shallow depression on bog or upland. 4 eggs.

Egg: Actual Size

White-rumped Sandpiper
Calidris fuscicollis

Observation Calendar

J F M A M J J A S O N D

Male/Female: *Spring and Summer*: Light grey and rufous brown speckled with darker browns on head, back and wings; chest speckled lighter buff fading to white on belly; bill black with red underside; tail and wing tips dark brown and black; feet and legs black. *Winter*: Colours change to grey overall. *In flight*: White rump; white under wings.

Voice: Call is high-pitched *jeeeeeet* and *twitter*.
Food: Crustaceans, worms, snails, insects.

Purple Sandpiper
Calidris maritima

Observation Calendar
J F M A M J J A S O N D

Male/Female: *Winter:* Overall soft grey with dark brown spots and rust; chest fades to pale belly; orange bill is slightly curved down which becomes black at end; dark eye with white eye-ring; legs and feet yellow/orange. *In flight:* White wing band; white rump on sides; dark underparts.

Voice: Call is a *twheeeet* and *twiiit*.
Food: Crustaceans, molluscs, insects, seeds and algae.

Dunlin

Calidris alpina

Observation Calendar

J F M A M J J A S O N D

Male/Female: Long black bill; grey face with rust and black speckled crown; breast white speckled brown; dull brown wings and back; short black tail; feet and legs black. *In flight:* White underparts and wing feathers.

Did you know? Dunlins usually flock together performing wonderful aerial shows when flushed.

Voice: *In flight* call: soft *creeeep* or *chit-lit.*
Food: Crustaceans, molluscs, marine worms, insects.

Short-billed Dowitcher

Limnodromus griseus

Observation Calendar
J F M A M J J A S O N D

Male/Female: *Summer*: Rust neck and chest speckled black; back and wings dark brown speckled with buff; dark brown cap on head. *Winter*: Grey speckled overall with dark, barred flanks; black bill fading to yellow near base, white eyebrows; black and brown tail feathers; feet and legs yellow.

Voice: Call is *tu*, repeated several times in soft high-pitch.
Food: Marine worms, molluscs, insects

Common Snipe
Gallinago gallinago

Observation Calendar

J F M A M J J A S O N D

Male/Female: Very long narrow bill; with small head and large brown/black eye; buff eye ring; black and white bars on white belly; brown back striped with pale yellow; short yellow feet and legs; tail has rust band. *In flight:* Pointed wings; flies in back and forth motion with quick wingbeats.

Did you know? The Common Snipe uses its long bill to hunt in bog-like conditions where it can penetrate through the soft ground to catch prey below the surface.

Voice: Call is a *swheet swheet* with sharp *scaip* call when flushed.
Food: Larvae, crayfish, molluscs, insects, frogs and seeds.
Nest/Eggs: Hollow in marsh area, concealed with grass, leaves, twigs and moss. 4 eggs.

Wilson's Phalarope

Phalaropus tricolor

Observation Calendar

J F M A M J J A S O N D

Male: *Summer*: White throat; light rust on back of head changing to pale grey on breast; pale grey underparts; grey back and wings.

Female: *Summer*: Long thin black bill, white chin and cheeks turning rust running down white neck; black band runs from beak through eye down side of neck to back; grey cap; white sides and belly; grey feet and legs. *In flight*: White rump; no wing bands; long legs.

Male/Female: *Winter*: Similar to summer male with pale grey, not rust, on head and neck.

Did you know? This is one species where the male does all the nest tending. He builds the nest, incubates eggs and raises young.

Voice: Soft call is *aangh*.
Food: Insects, crustaceans.
Nest/Eggs: Colonies. Hollow scrap on ground lined with grasses and concealed in grass. 4 eggs.

Red-necked Phalarope

Phalaropus lobatus

Observation Calendar

J F M A M J J A S O N D

Male/Female: *Winter*: White and grey chest and belly. Face white with black mark behind eye; dark grey wings and back.
Male: *Summer:* Top of head black; long black bill; white chin; black band running under eye against white and rust; rust neck; grey chest changing to white belly; dark brown and rust wings and back; tail black; white rump.

Female: Overall similar markings except bolder colour; and rufous neck with more contrast overall.

Voice: Call is sharp *twic.*
Food: Aquatic insects, molluscs, crustaceans.

Red Phalarope
Phalaropus fulicaria

Observation Calendar
J F M A M J J A S O N D

Male: *Summer*: Black cap and white mask over eye to back of head; yellow bill with black tip; body rust red with grey belly; wings brown with tan highlights.
Female: *Summer*: Bright yellow bill with black tip; black head with large white patch around eye to back of neck; long rufous neck, rufous chest, belly and sides; black back with white and rust highlights; rufous rump. *In flight*: White wing band on underside.
Male/Female: *Winter*: White and pale grey head, neck, breast and belly; back and wings grey; black mark over eye.

Voice: Call is high-pitched *wiiit* or *kreep*.
Food: Aquatic insects, small fish, crustaceans.

Yellow Rail
Coturnicops noveboracensis

Size Identification

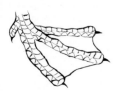

Foot: Anisodactyl

Flying

Feeding

Observation Calendar
J F M A M J J A S O N D

Male/Female: Chicken-like; dark band running across top of head to back; thick yellow bill; dark brown running through eye; buff face, breast and belly; dark brown and buff on back and wings with white bars. *In flight*: White patch on edge of wings.

Voice: Call a progressive *click click click* similar to tapping two stones together.
Food: Snails, insects, seeds.
Nest/Eggs: Well concealed cup built into grass or attached to stems slightly above water level. 7-10 eggs.

Egg: Actual Size

Virginia Rail
Rallus limicola

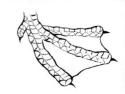

Foot: Anisodactyl

Flying

Feeding

Observation Calendar

J F M A M J J A S O N D

Male/Female: Chicken-like; grey head banded dark charcoal on top; eye red; neck and sides rich rust; long curved red and black bill; back dark brown with rust edging; wings rust with black; short black and brown tail; legs and feet red; belly black and white banding.

Voice: Call is descending *kicket* repeated with grunting notes.
Food: Marine worms, snails, aquatic insects.
Nest/Eggs: Cup built of grass and reeds built slightly above water's surface attached to reeds and other aquatic plant life. 5-12 eggs.

Egg: Actual Size

Sora
Porzana carolina

Size Identification

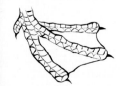

Foot: Anisodactyl

Flying

Observation Calendar
J F M A M J J A S O N D

Feeding

Male/Female: Chicken-like; grey above eye runs down to chin, breast and belly; black mask behind thick yellow bill; upper parts chestnut brown with white and dark brown bars; legs and feet yellow; buff rump.

Did you know? The Sora, like other rails, prefers to migrate at night.

Voice: Call is musical *kuur weeee* which is repeated and descends.
Food: Aquatic insects and seeds.
Nest/Eggs: Built in open marsh, attached to reeds, using leaves and grass. 6-15 eggs.

Egg: Actual Size

Inland Birds

Many of the 125 inland birds selected here can be seen anywhere in the province. In woodland and meadows, where songbirds and other small species such as chickadees, finches, flycatchers, nuthatches, sparrows and warblers abound, you are also likely to see hawks and other raptors.

In wilderness areas, especially in national and provincial parks, where habitat is less disturbed by human activity, there are opportunities to see and hear specific uncommon species. Park interpreters can provide specific information on the birds and hot spot areas to be found in each park.

Many species have adapted well to urban settings. In parks and suburban areas, you can see a wide variety of year-round inhabitants. Birds can be attracted to your backyard by the type of trees, bushes and plants that are growing there. This book indicates those that will come to a backyard bird feeder and those that will make use of a nesting box. One popular summer visitor, the Ruby-throated Hummingbird, can often be seen hovering in flower gardens and at specially designed hummingbird feeders.

The visual keys in this section depict seasonal range — when you will see the bird — its size, the type of foot and the nesting location. The egg is shown for birds that breed in the province. The description emphasizes the distinctive markings of each bird, the food preferences and the calls or songs of each bird.

Killdeer
Charadrius vociferus

Observation Calendar

J F M A M J J A S O N D

Male/Female: Bright red eye with black band running across forehead; white chin, collar and eyebrow; black collar ring under white; black chest band set against white chest and belly; back and wing rust and grey; wing tipped in black; legs and feet pink/grey. *In flight*: Orange rump; black wing tips and white band on trailing edge.

Did you know? A killdeer will exhibit a "broken-wing" display when a predator comes close to the nest sight. The bird will appear hurt and run around distracting the predator from the nest.

Voice: Variety of calls with most common being *kill deeee* which is repeated.
Food: Insects.
Nest/Eggs: Hollow on ground with some pebbles. Most popular sightings in gravel parking lots. 3-4 eggs.

American Woodcock

Scolopax minor

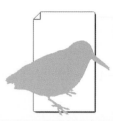

Observation Calendar

J F M A M J J A S O N D

Male/Female: Distinctive long, straight, narrow bill of light brown; large brown eyes set back on the head; overall brown-black back with buff underside; feet and legs pale pink. *In flight*: Short wings explode with clatter.

Did you know? When courtship is taking place, the males will rise up in the air and circle around as high as 15 metres.

Voice: A deep *peeeeint* and a tin whistle sounding twitter when in flight.
Food: Earthworms, a variety of insects and insect larvae and seeds.
Nest/Eggs: Shallow depression on ground lined with dead leaves and needles, in wooded area. 4 eggs.

Gray Partridge
Perdix perdix

Size Identification

Foot: Anisodactyl

Egg: Actual Size

Observation Calendar
J F M A M J J A S O N D

Male/Female: Overall grey with brick red face and throat, reddish brown banding on wings, feet and legs yellow; bill pale yellow. *In flight:* Brick red tail feathers are exposed.

Did you know? These game birds were introduced to North America from Europe.

Voice: Call is a *keee ukk.*
Food: A variety of seeds, grain, leaves and insects.
Nest/Eggs: Hollow in ground, in thick wooded areas, under felled log or rock, lined with leaves, pine needles and feathers. 9-12 eggs.

Nesting Location

Ring-necked Pheasant

Phasianus colchicus

Size Identification

Foot: Anisodactyl

Egg: 80%

Observation Calendar

J F M A M J J A S O N D

Male: Green iridescent head with distinctive red wattles (patches around eye), white collar, overall body is mixture of grey, black and brown; long tail feathers brown with black banding; feet and legs charcoal grey; pale yellow bill.
Female: Grey-brown overall with dark markers over entire body; pale yellow bill; small red wattle above eye.

Did you know? This chicken-like bird gets into some real cock fights in early spring, jumping, pecking, clawing for their right to territory.

Voice: Similar to a wild turkey gobble at a higher pitch.
Food: Seeds, insects, grains and berries.
Nest/Eggs: Shallow bowl on ground lined with weed, grass and leaves. 6-15 eggs.

Backyard Feeder

Nesting Location

Ruffed Grouse

Bonasa umbellus

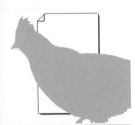

Size Identification

Foot: Anisodactyl

Egg: Actual Size

Observation Calendar

J F M A M J J A S O N D

Male: Distinctive crest on head; overall brown speckled bird with black shoulder band on back of neck; tail is grey with broad black band at tip; eye brown; feet and legs grey.
Female: Similar to male except browner and more barring on underside; black shoulder band is narrower.

Did you know? The female will act injured if there is a threat near the nest.

Voice: An alarm note of *qit qit*. Cooing by female.
Food: A variety of insects, seeds, tree buds, leaves and berries.
Nest/Eggs: Hollow under log or near the base of a tree lined with leaves, pine needles and feathers. 9-12 eggs.

Nesting Location

Spruce Grouse

Falcipennis canadensis

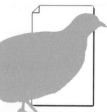
Size Identification

Foot: Anisodactyl

Egg: Actual Size

Observation Calendar

J F M A M J J A S O N D

Male: Black chest and chin; overall black speckled with larger white areas on front; feet and legs charcoal; red head patch; small black curved bill; tail black with brown tips.
Female: Similar to male overall except black is replaced with brown or grey.

Did you know? A trademark for grouse is the drumming sound they can create by quick beating of their wings that is done in courtship or territorial display.

Voice: Mostly silent birds with occasional hissing.
Food: Ground insects, buds of conifers, wild berries, a variety of seeds.
Nest/Eggs: Hollow on ground lined with dead leaves, grass, pine needles and feathers, preferring locations under conifers and in tangled bushes. 4-10 eggs.

Nesting Location

Common Nighthawk
Chordeiles minor

Observation Calendar

J F M A M J J A S O N D

Male: Grey and black speckled bird with long thin wings; white collar wraps around to bottom of neck; legs and feet light grey. When in flight white bands near tail are visible.

Did you know? This bird eats in flight by scooping insects into their large mouths. You can often see nighthawks feeding near lights on warm nights.

Voice: A nasal sounding *peeent*.
Food: Flying insects.
Nest/Eggs: In depression on the ground, often in gravel, with lining. 2 eggs.

Whip-poor-will
Caprimulgus vociferus

Observation Calendar

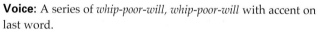

J F M A M J J A S O N D

Male/Female: Grey fluffy bird with brown cheeks; short black rounded wings; short tail; black bill lightly covered with feathers; large black eyes.

Voice: A series of *whip-poor-will, whip-poor-will* with accent on last word.
Food: Flying insects including moths, beetles and grasshoppers.
Nest/Eggs: Depression of dead leaves on the ground formed around eggs. 2 eggs.

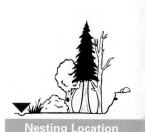

101

Osprey
Pandion haliaetus

Size Identification

Foot: Zygodactyl

Egg: 70%

Observation Calendar

J F M A M J J A S O N D

Male/Female: *In flight*: White belly and chest; wings grey with black banding; white wing underparts connect to chest; black band running through eye; large black bill; tail grey with black banding. *Perched*: Black back and wings with thin white line running above wing; eye yellow with black band running through and down to cheek; chin white; top of head white with black patches.
Female: More streaked then males.

Voice: A loud chirp which trails off or ascending *squeeeee* during courtship displays.
Food: Various small fish.
Nest/Eggs: Constructed of twigs and sticks, lined with sod, grass and vines in upper parts of trees and on top of poles, 60 feet above ground 2-3 eggs.

Nesting Location

Bald Eagle

Haliaeetus leucocephalus

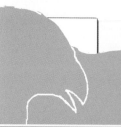

Size Identification

Foot: Anisodactyl

Egg: 75%

Observation Calendar

J F M A M J J A S O N D

Male/Female: *In flight*: Broad black wings and belly with white head and tail feathers. *Perched*: White head with brilliant yellow eyes, white tail feathers, black back and wings, feet and legs yellow; bill yellow.
Juvenile: Mistaken for Golden Eagle because it lacks white head and tail; chest, white and speckled; black wings with white speckles; underparts black with large areas of white.

Did you know? The eagle population is now recovering from rapid declines in the 1970s due to the widespread use of DDT.

Voice: A loud scream given in multiples.
Food: A variety of small and medium-sized mammals, fish and carrion.
Nest/Eggs: Upper parts of large, often dead, trees built with large twigs, lined with grass, moss, sod and weeds. 2 eggs.

Nesting Location

Size Identification

Foot: Anisodactyl

Egg: 90%

Northern Harrier (Marsh Hawk)

Circus cyaneus

Observation Calendar

J F M A M J J A S O N D

Male: *In flight*: White underside with black and rust speckles; head is grey; black on tips of wings; orange feet; wings are V-shaped in flight. *Perched*: Grey head with white face mask; yellow eyes; thin rust banding down front; white rump.
Female: Slightly larger than male with brown overall; buff face disk around cheeks; buff under chin and belly is banded with brown; bill grey; yellow eyes.

Did you know? While gliding over meadows, the Northern Harrier's wings take a V-shape, making it easy to identify.

Voice: Relatively quiet bird with occasional screams of alarm.
Food: A variety of small mammals and birds.
Nest/Eggs: On or near ground, built of sticks, straw and grasses. 4-5 eggs.

Nesting Location

104

Sharp-shinned Hawk

Accipiter striatus

Foot: Anisodactyl

Egg: Actual Size

Observation Calendar

J F M A M J J A S O N D

Male/Female: *In flight*: Small hawk with rust chest banded with buff; long square tail is white with charcoal banding; wings dark brown and rounded; top of head dark brown. *Perched*: Brick-red eyes with brown band just below eye; bill is black with yellow base; feet and legs yellow; white feathers extend out of rust coloured belly.

Did you know? Over the past few years there has been a dramatic decrease in the eastern population. This may be directly related to the decrease in songbirds that it hunts.

Voice: A quick high pitched *kik kik kik*.
Food: Small songbirds.
Nest/Eggs: Broad platforms of twigs and sticks in conifers or deciduous trees built against the trunk, lined with bark. 4-5 eggs.

Nesting Location

Cooper's Hawk
Accipiter cooperii

Observation Calendar

J F M A M J J A S O N D

Male/Female: *In flight*: White chest and belly with rust banding down to lower belly; buff tail is long and rounded with faint charcoal banding; chin white; buff and white under wings with charcoal banding; grey on top of head. When in flight it has a steady wingbeat. *Perched*: Grey wings and tail with rust edging at ends; eyes are brick red; bill black and yellow; feet and legs yellow with rust feathers banded white down to knee.

Voice: Call is a loud *kek kek kek*.
Food: Small birds.
Nest/Eggs: Large nest built of sticks and twigs, in conifer tree, 6-18 metres above ground. 4-5 eggs.

Northern Goshawk

Accipiter gentilis

Foot: Anisodactyl

Egg: 80%

Observation Calendar

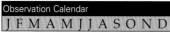

J F M A M J J A S O N D

Male/Female: *In flight*: Underside is grey with dark brown banding overall; tail long with rich red along edges; buff eyebrow runs to back of neck. *Perched*: Dark brown wings with buff edging; eye brick red; bill black with yellow at base; feet and legs yellow with white feathers, banded brown reaching down to knees.

Did you know? This is an aggressive bird that has the ability fly in densely wooded areas chasing small birds.

Voice: Loud *keeek keeek keeek.*
Food: Small birds and occasional small mammals, such as squirrels.
Nest/Eggs: Stick nest lodged in crotch of tree against the trunk, lined with bark, feathers and down. 3-4 eggs.

Nesting Location

Red-shouldered Hawk

Buteo lineatus

Size Identification

Foot: Anisodactyl

Egg: 75%

Observation Calendar
J F M A M J J A S O N D

Male/Female: *In flight*: Rust red chest lightly banded with buff, pale crescent on outer area of wings. *Perched*: Red brick shoulder patch; black wings with streaks of white; head buff with dark brown streaking; tail dark with white banding; bill black with yellow at base, feet and legs yellow with buff feathers banded with rust that reach just above feet; eyes dark.

Did you know? Red-shouldered Hawks return to the same nesting site year after year.

Voice: Decreasing scream *ke-er-ke-er-ke-er*.
Food: Amphibians, snakes, small mammals, small birds and insects.
Nest/Eggs: Sticks and twigs lined with bark, feathers and down, built close to trunk in cavity of tree, near swamps and bogs. 3 eggs.

Nesting Location

Broad-winged Hawk

Buteo platypterus

Foot: Anisodactyl

Egg: 70%

Observation Calendar

J F M A M J J A S O N D

Male/Female: *In flight*: Brownish red banding on chest and belly; wings white with faint banding; tail broad with large black banding against white; chin white; top of head brown. *Perched*: Dark brown wings; yellow eye ringed in black; feet and legs yellow; bill charcoal grey.

Did you know? In September hawks sometimes gather together in flocks of hundreds.

Voice: Whistle that is high-pitched *peee peeeeee*.
Food: Small mammals, birds, reptiles and amphibians.
Nest/Eggs: Small stick, twigs, and leaves, lined with bark, in main supporting branches of tree, against trunk. 2-3 eggs.

Nesting Location

Red-tailed Hawk
Buteo jamaicensis

Size Identification

Foot: Anisodactyl

Egg: 75%

Observation Calendar

J F M A M J J A S O N D

Male/Female: *In flight*: Tail will appear faint red depending on light; broad wings and belly, white banded with charcoal. *Perched*: Wings are dark brown with buff edges; eyes brick red; bill yellow and black; feet and legs yellow with white feathers banded brown/charcoal reach to knees; tail brick red.

Voice: A scream that is downward *keeer er er*.
Food: Small mammals, amphibians, nestlings, insects, reptiles and birds.
Nest/Eggs: Flat and shallow, stick and twig nest, lined with moss and evergreen sprigs, on rocky ledges or in trees that are in the open, 10-30 metres above ground. 2 eggs.

Nesting Location

Rough-legged Hawk

Buteo lagopus

Size Identification

Foot: Anisodactyl

Egg: 65%

Observation Calendar
J F M A M J J A S O N D

Male/Female: *In-flight*: Dark patches on white belly with banding; black patch at wrist of underwing; white tail with one dark band at tip. *Perched*: Dark brown wings with buff head that is banded with dark brown; yellow eyes; base of tail white rump; black bill, yellow at base; yellow feet and legs with buff feathers that are banded brown to knees.

Voice: A whistle along with a *keeeerrr* that descends.
Food: Small rodents.
Nest/Eggs: Stick nest in tree. 2-4 eggs.

Nesting Location

American Kestrel
Falco sparverius

Size Identification

Foot: Anisodactyl

Egg: Actual Size

Observation Calendar

J F M A M J J A S O N D

Male/Female: *In flight*: Overall buff with black speckles; distinctive black banding on face. *Perched*: charcoal wings with black, separated banding; back rust with black banding; grey top of head with rust patch on top; black bands running down cheeks against white; bill black/charcoal with yellow at base; feet and legs orange; tail deep rust with broad black tip.

Voice: Rapid *klee klee klee* or *kily kily kily*.
Food: Mice, voles, insects and small birds.
Nest/Eggs: In cavity of tree or man-made boxes, little or no nesting material. 3-5 eggs.

Nesting Location

Merlin
Falco columbarius

Foot: Anisodactyl

Egg: Actual Size

Observation Calendar

J F M A M J J A S O N D

Male: *In flight*: Buff underside with dark brown banding overall; dark brown head with thin buff eyebrow; tail dark. *Perched*: Slate-blue wings with slight amount of white edges; bill black with yellow at base; feet and legs pale yellow.
Female: Brown back and wings; buff underparts with brown streaks.

Did you know? Often called the "bullet hawk," this is a very fast bird when racing after its prey. It has a wonderful ability to turn quickly and accelerate in flight, even through thick woods.

Voice: Rapid and high-pitched *clee clee clee*.
Food: Small birds in flight, reptiles, amphibians and insects.
Nest/Eggs: Stick interwoven with moss, twigs, lichen and conifer needles, on cliff ledge or cavity of tree. 4-5 eggs.

Nesting Location

Peregrine Falcon
Falco peregrinus

Observation Calendar

J F M A M J J A S O N D

Male/Female: *In flight*: Overall white underside with charcoal banding; face has black mask and sideburns with yellow around dark eyes, bill is yellow and grey, feet and legs are yellow. *Perched*: Black wings with buff edging on feathers.

Did you know? The Peregrine can reach the fastest speeds of any animal on earth — 260 km/h.

Voice: A series of high pitched screams *ki ki ki.*
Food: Catches birds in flight and occasionally will eat larger insects.
Nest/Eggs: Slight hollow in rock ledge or flat roof top, built with sticks. 3-5 eggs.

Great Horned Owl

Bubo virginianus

Size Identification

Foot: Zygodactyl

Egg: 70%

Observation Calendar

J F M A M J J A S O N D

Male/Female: Very recognizable ear tufts that sit wide apart; bright yellow eyes surrounded by rust colour; grey and brown overall with black bands.

Voice: Hoot consists of several *hoo hoo hoo hoo hoo hoo*. Male is deeper then female.

Food: Small mammals, birds and reptiles.

Nest/Eggs: Nests in a deserted hawk's, heron's or crow's nest with very little material added. Occasionally will lay eggs on ground amongst bones, skulls and bits of fur. 1-3 eggs.

Nesting Location

Barred Owl

Strix varia

Size Identification

Foot: Zygodactyl

Egg: 60%

Observation Calendar
J F M A M J J A S O N D

Male/Female: Large dark eyes set in buff and rich brown; white bands extend out from face, down the back including wings and tail feathers; chest white with rich brown feathers in columns; bill is small yellow hook shape.

Did you know? The Barred Owls' ears are positioned differently on either side of the head. This allows for better hearing in total darkness.

Voice: Very rhythmic hoots in series of four or five at a time.
Food: Small mammals
Nest/Eggs: Cavity of tree or abandoned hawksÌ or crowsÌ nests; no lining added. 2-3 eggs.

Nesting Location

Short-eared Owl

Asio flammeus

Observation Calendar

J F M A M J J A S O N D

Male/Female: Dark brown overall with buff banding on back; small ear tufts black and buff directly above eyes on top of head (rarely seen); wings and tail feathers dark brown with buff bands; light buff chest and belly with brown streaks; long wings tipped black at the ends; eyes brilliant yellow surrounded by black; bill black; feet and legs black.

Did you know? The Short-eared Owl flies low to the ground when hunting but is able to hover momentarily when prey is spotted.

Voice: Raspy *yip yip yip*.
Food: Small mammals, mostly voles, songbirds and game birds.
Nest/Eggs: Slight depression hidden in grass. Lined with grass and feathers. 4-9 eggs.

Northern Saw-whet Owl

Aegolius acadicus

Size Identification

Foot: Zygodactyl

Egg: Actual Size

Observation Calendar

J F M A M J J A S O N D

Male/Female: Yellow eyes that are surrounded by a reddish brown facial disk; chest white with brown streaks running length of body; feet and legs grey.

Voice: Whistled song repeated *too too too.*
Food: Diet consists mainly of small mammals, including voles, chipmunks, and bats.
Nest/Eggs: Cavity of dead tree, 4-18 metres above ground. No material added. 2-6 eggs.

Nesting Location

Rock Dove (Pigeon)
Columba livia

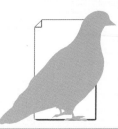

Size Identification

Foot: Anisodactyl

Egg: Actual Size

Observation Calendar

J F M A M J J A S O N D

Male/Female: Varies greatly from solid white to solid black and everything in between. Most birds have dark grey head with hints of iridescent colours along the neck; body light grey with two charcoal wing bands; tail and wings dark grey with black bands; rump is white.

Did you know? Pigeons were introduced to North America in the 1800s. They are now prevalent everywhere, especially in urban areas.

Backyard Feeder

Voice: Soft descending *kooooo kooooo.*
Food: Seeds and grain
Nest/Eggs: Flimsy nest of twigs, grass, straw and debris, on ledges or crevices of buildings and bridges, in colonies. 1-2 eggs.

Nesting Location

119

Mourning Dove
Zenaida macroura

Size Identification

Foot: Anisodactyl

Egg: Actual Size

Backyard Feeder

Observation Calendar

J F M A M J J A S O N D

Male: Buff coloured head and body; dark grey wings and tail; bill is black with speckles of red at opening; wings have small black feathers highlighted against softer grey, eyes black surrounded by light blue; feet and legs red; tail is long and pointed.
Female: Similar except for head, neck and chest are evenly brown.

Did you know? When the mourning dove is in flight its wings whistle.

Voice: Very distinct cooing sound that sounds a little sad, *coooahooo oo oo oo* fading at the end.
Food: A variety of seeds and grain
Nest/Eggs: Platform of sticks and twigs, lined with grass and rootlets, in evergreens, 15 metres above ground. 1-2 eggs.

Nesting Location

Black-billed Cuckoo
Coccyzus erythropthalmus

Foot: Anisodactyl

Egg: Actual Size

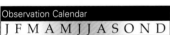

Observation Calendar
J F M A M J J A S O N D

Male/Female: Distinct black beak curved slightly downward; red ring around black eyes; upper body parts brown; wings brown; long tail with 3 white spots on underside; white chin, chest and belly; feet and legs charcoal grey.

Did you know? The Black-billed Cuckoo is an important species for farmers since much of its diet consists of caterpillars, which are destructive to plants.

Voice: Softly repeated *cu cu cu cu cu* in groups of 2-5 at the same pitch.
Food: Insects, lizards, mollusks, fishes, frogs and berries.
Nest/Eggs: Shallow, built of twigs and grasses and lined with softer materials including ferns, roots and plant-down; usually built near tree trunk in dense area. 2-5 eggs.

Nesting Location

Red-headed Woodpecker
Melanerpes erythrocephalus

Size Identification

Foot: Zygodactyl

Egg: Actual Size

Backyard Feeder

Nesting Location

Observation Calendar
J F M A M J J A S O N D

Male/Female: Bright red hood over head with grey and black bill; back is black with large distinctive white patches on wings; feet and legs grey; tail feathers are pointed and black; chest and belly white.

Did you know? These woodpeckers are declining because of forestry practices and are competing unsuccessfully with European starlings for nesting locations.

Voice: Call is a deep hoarse *queer queeeer queeer*.
Food: A variety of insects and insect larvae.
Nest/Eggs: Cavity of tree with no added material, 2 -25 metres above ground. 4-7 eggs.

Downy Woodpecker

Picoides pubescens

Foot: Zygodactyl

Observation Calendar
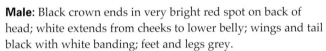
J F M A M J J A S O N D

Egg: Actual Size

Male: Black crown ends in very bright red spot on back of head; white extends from cheeks to lower belly; wings and tail black with white banding; feet and legs grey.
Female: Similar except without red spot on back of head.

Voice: Whiny call and a *queek, queek* call during courtship. Listen for bird pounding on trees looking for insects.
Food: Larvae and other tree-dwelling insects.
Nest/Eggs: Cavity for nest excavated in decaying trees, 1-5 metres above ground. 3-6 eggs.

Backyard Feeder

Nesting Location

Hairy Woodpecker

Picoides villosus

Size Identification

Foot: Zygodactyl

Egg: Actual Size

Backyard Feeder

Observation Calendar

J F M A M J J A S O N D

Male/Female: Black head with white banding along cheek and through eye; white back and underparts; wings and tail black with white spotting; feet and legs charcoal grey; bill is nearly length of head; outer tail feathers white.

Voice: A bright sounding *peek...peek* which may be followed by a rattling call. *Wickiwickiwicki* call during courtship.
Food: Larvae, wood-boring insects. At feeders suet and wildflower seeds.
Nest/Eggs: Cavity for nest excavated in live trees, 1-5 metres above ground. 4-6 eggs.

Nesting Location

Black-backed Woodpecker

Picoides arcticus

Foot: Zygodactyl

Observation Calendar

J F M A M J J A S O N D

Male: Black head with a definite yellow crown on top; back, wings and tail black with occasional bands of white at ends; throat, neck and belly white with speckles; feet and legs grey; black bill is long and thin
Female: Similar to male except no yellow crown on top of head.

Egg: Actual Size

Did you know? The Black-backed Woodpecker has a tendency to rip large portions of bark off trees excavating for food.

Voice: Very shrill cries, similar to *kiiiik*. Easiest sound to identify is the pounding on trees either excavating for a nest or foraging for food.
Food: Larvae, wood boring beetles, fruits, nuts and a variety of other insects.
Nest/Eggs: Cavity of tree with no added material, .5-5 metres feet above ground. 2-6 eggs.

Nesting Location

Northern Flicker

Colaptes auratus

Observation Calendar
J F M A M J J A S O N D

Male: Grey at top of head which stops at bright red spot on back of neck; black eye is encircled in light brown, with a black line running off bill to lower neck; chest begins with black half-moon necklace on front and turns into a white belly with black spots; wings and tail greyish-brown with black banding; white rump; yellow feathers are evident under sharp pointed tail feathers while in flight.
Female: Similar to male except without the black line running from bill.

Voice: Various sounds depending on its use. When claiming its territory a series of *kekekekeke* and when in courtship *woeka-woeka-woeka*.
Food: Digs and pokes on the ground looking for ants and other insects, fruit and seeds. Most of its diet consists of ants.
Nest/Eggs: Cavity of tree with no added material, .5-18 metres above ground. 3-10 eggs.

Pileated Woodpecker

Dryocopus pileatus

Foot: Zygodactyl

Egg: Actual Size

Observation Calendar

J F M A M J J A S O N D

Male: Crow-sized woodpecker with a distinctive red crest at top; red band running from black bill to cheek; black extends down neck to tail; cheeks and throat have white banding. In flight, white patches are visible on wings; feet and legs black.
Female: Black forehead replaces portion of red crest. No red band from bill to cheek.

Did you know? The Pileated Woodpecker can be so aggressive when chiseling away at trees that it can weaken the tree to falling point.

Backyard Feeder

Voice: A quick set of calls, *whucker, whucker, whucker,* in duets sometimes followed by a sharp *kuk* when contacting mate.
Food: Larvae, ants and tree-dwelling insects, wild fruits, acorns and beechnuts.
Nest/Eggs: Cavity of tree with no added material. 3-4 eggs.

Nesting Location

Size Identification

Foot: Anisodactyl

Red-breasted Nuthatch

Sitta canadensis

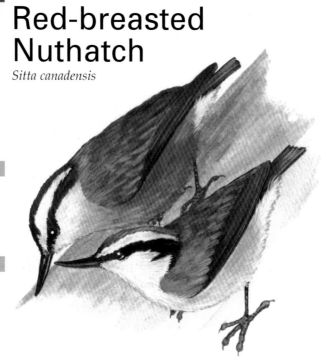

Egg: Actual Size

Observation Calendar
J F M A M J J A S O N D

Male: Small round bird with black stripe over top of head and white stripe underneath running over eye to back of head, followed by another black band running through eye; white cheeks turn to rust at neck and continue rust to chest and belly; back is grey-blue; wings and tail grey becoming black at ends; black bill is often white on underside; feet and legs brown-black.
Female: Similar to male except for grey cap and light underside.

Backyard Feeder

Did you know? The Red-breasted Nuthatch will smear pitch at the entrance to its nest, although it is not known why.

Birdhouse Nester

Voice: A tin-whistle call and an occasional loud *knack knack.*
Food: Seeds, insects and flying insects
Nest/Eggs: Cup lined with grass, moss and feathers, in excavated cavity or crevice of tree. 1-12 metres above ground. 4-7 eggs.

Nesting Location

128

White-breasted Nuthatch

Sitta carolinensis

Size Identification

Foot: Anisodactyl

J F M A M J J A S O N D

Male: Shiny black on top of head running down the back, turning to lighter blue-grey on back; white face and neck which runs down chest and belly; slight rust colours on sides, wings and tail are blue-grey with white edges; feet and legs black.

Female: Similar to male except top of head and back are lighter grey.

Did you know? These little birds are known for their ability to run down tree trunks headfirst, at a very fast pace.

Voice: Nesting pairs keep in contact with one another with a deep sounding *aank aank* but also chatter a soft *ip ip*.

Food: Spiders, insects, seeds, insect eggs and acorns.

Nest/Eggs: Cup lined with twig, feathers, small roots, fur and hair, in natural cavity or crevice of tree, 4-15 metres above ground. 5-10 eggs.

Egg: Actual Size

Backyard Feeder

Birdhouse Nester

Nesting Location

129

Brown Creeper

Certhia americana

Size Identification

Foot: Anisodactyl

Egg: Actual Size

Backyard Feeder

Observation Calendar
J F M A M J J A S O N D

Male/Female: Overall brown with grey streaks and white chin, chest and belly; long curved bill that is black on top and white/pink on bottom; distinctive eye stripe; feet and legs grey; tail is long and pointed.

Did you know? Spending most of its day creeping up and down trees looking for meals, the Brown Creeper can flatten itself and blend into the colour of the tree trunk when a predator passes by.

Voice: A very high whistling *see wee see tu eee.*
Food: Insects, insect and spider eggs and occasionally nuts and seeds.
Nest/Eggs: Cup with foundation of twig, bark, and leaves, lined with bark, grass, feathers and moss, in cavity or under loose bark of tree, up to 5 metres above ground. 4-8 eggs.

Nesting Location

Chimney Swift

Chaetura pelagica

Size Identification

Foot: Anisodactyl

Observation Calendar

J F M A M J J A S O N D

Male/Female: Dark charcoal on head, back, wings and tail; lighter on chest and throat; black bill is small with light grey on underside; feet and legs grey.

Egg: Actual Size

Did you know? A Chimney Swift is capable of snapping off tree twigs with its feet while in flight. It then takes the twig in its mouth and returns to its nest.

Voice: A very quick and repeated *chitter, chitter, chitter* with occasional *chip*.
Food: Flying insects such as moths and beetles.
Nest/Eggs: Flimsy half cup attached by saliva to crevice or rock ledge in chimneys, barns, old buildings, and on rock formations. 3-6 eggs.

Nesting Location

Purple Martin

Progne subis

Observation Calendar

J F M A M J J A S O N D

Male: Very shiny, dark purple overall, with black wings and tail; black bill is short and slightly curved; feet and legs reddish black; wings very long reaching to tip of tail when folded.
Female: Dull purple head and back with black wings and tail; chest and chin grey; belly white with black speckles; feet and legs black.

Voice: Call is high pitched *cheer cheer.*
Food: Flying insects.
Nest/Eggs: Deep cup in cavity lined with grass and leaves, usually in large colonies. Nests in gourds and special martin houses. 3-8 eggs.

Tree Swallow

Tachycineta bicolor

Foot: Anisodactyl

Observation Calendar
J F M A M J J A S O N D

Male/Female: Dark iridescent blue on head, neck, back, wings and tail; bright white chin, chest and belly; black bill is short and slightly curved; wings are very long reaching down to tip of tail when folded; feet and legs charcoal.

Egg: Actual Size

Did you know? The Tree Swallow is the only swallow that eats berries in the place of insects. This allows it to winter further north than its relatives.

Voice: Early morning song *wheet trit weet*, with an alarm call of *cheedeeep*.
Food: Flying insects and berries.
Nest/Eggs: Cup in cavity of tree lined with grass and feathers, usually a woodpecker's old hole. 4-6 eggs.

Birdhouse Nester

Nesting Location

Bank Swallow

Riparia riparia

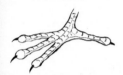

Observation Calendar

J F M A M J J A S O N D

Male/Female: Dirty brown overall with white front except for brown band running across chest; wings are very long reaching down to tip of tail when folded; feet and legs grey; black bill is short and curved.

Voice: A variety of calls including *tchirrt tchirrt* and long twittering.
Food: Flying insects as well as a variety of other insects. Main diet consists of dragonflies, flies, mayflies and beetles.
Nest/Eggs: Earth tunnel lined with grass and straw along bank of water. 4-6 eggs.

Cliff Swallow

Petrochelidon pyrrhonota

Size Identification

Foot: Anisodactyl

Observation Calendar

J F M A M J J A S O N D

Male/Female: Overall black with buff rump and brick red cheeks; white patch on forehead; belly white; back has variable amounts of white streaks; feet and legs grey; tail black, square at end.

Egg: Actual Size

Did you know? Nest sights can be a little competitive and the birds will steal nesting grasses and twigs from each other's nests.

Voice: A long *chuuurrrr* and a deeper *nyeeew*.
Food: A variety of insects.
Nest/Eggs: Mud lined with grass, hair and feathers, under bridges, in cliffs and buildings. 3-6 eggs.

Nesting Location

Barn Swallow
Hirundo rustica

Observation Calendar

J F M A M J J A S O N D

Male: Dark blue iridescent from top of head, shoulders, down back and top of wings; chin and chest rust colour that fades to white at belly; wings are very long and extend to tips of tail which is forked with long feathers at either end that can be seen when bird is in flight; feet and legs charcoal; black and cream bill. When bird is in flight a band of white can be seen at end of wings.

Female: Same markings but duller.

Did you know? Barn Swallows are amazing to watch as they skim over water and pick insects off the surface. In the evening they hunt mosquitoes.

Voice: A soft twittering *kvik kvik wit wit*.

Food: A variety of insects.

Nest/Eggs: Mud and straw lined with feathers, in buildings, under bridges, in cliffs and caves. 4-5 eggs.

Ruby-throated Hummingbird

Archilochus colubris

Size Identification

Foot: Anisodactyl

Male: Dark green head which is iridescent in parts; red throat begins darker under chin; white collar, breast and belly; wings and notched tail black; iridescent green on back; black bill is long and thin; small white area behind eyes; feet and legs black.
Female: Head, back and parts of tail are bright iridescent green; white throat, chest and belly; wings and tail black with white outer tips; black bill is long and thin; small white area behind eyes; feet and legs black.

Voice: A low *hummmmmm* followed occasionally by a angry sounding squeak or chattering.
Food: Nectar from a variety of plants including thistles, jewel-weed, trumpet vines and other blossoms, occasionally insects.
Nest/Eggs: Small, tightly woven cup with deep cavity built with fibres and attached with spider web, lined with plant down, covered on the outside with lichens, in tree or shrub, 3-6 metres above ground. 2 eggs.

Egg: Actual Size

Backyard Feeder

Nesting Location

137

Belted Kingfisher

Ceryle alcyon

Observation Calendar

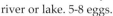
J F M A M J J A S O N D

Male: A large head and long black bill, crested blue/black head, very short blue tail; wings black with white bands; chest white; white collar wraps around neck with blue band that wraps around chest; feet and legs charcoal.
Female: Same as male except a rust colour breast band.

Did you know? Belted Kingfishers teach their young to dive for food by catching a fish, stunning it, then placing it on the surface of the water. The young birds then practise diving for it.

Voice: A continuous deep rattle during flight.
Food: Small fish, amphibians, reptiles, insects and crayfish.
Nest/Eggs: A cavity or tunnel excavated in a bank near a river or lake. 5-8 eggs.

Olive-sided Flycatcher

Contopus cooperi

Observation Calendar
J F M A M J J A S O N D

Male/Female: Dark grey/olive overall with crest at back of head; bar of white that runs down front from under chin to lower belly; white tufts on sides of rump but could be hidden by wings; feet and legs black; bill black on top with yellow underside.

Voice: a loud whistled hick, *three-bee-er* with first word quieter then others and the second is accented. A warning *chirp pip pip pip*.
Food: Flying insects.
Nest/Eggs: Flat cup attached to horizontal branch of conifer tree or shrub built with twigs, small roots and lichens and lined with pine needles and small roots, 2-15 metres above ground. 3 eggs.

Eastern Wood-Pewee
Contopus virens

Observation Calendar
J F M A M J J A S O N D

Male/Female: Olive-grey overall with head that is crested at back; wings black and dark grey with two white bars; throat and chest white; belly slightly yellow or white; tail charcoal; bill black on top and yellow underside; feet and legs black.

Did you know? The Wood-Pewee changes its voice in morning and evening, converting its song into a slow verse.

Voice: A soft whistle *pee-a-wee pee-awee* repeated without any pause early in the morning.
Food: Flies, beetles, bees, ants and other insects.
Nest/Eggs: Shallow cup built with grass, spider's web and fibres lined with hair, covered outside with lichens, on horizontal branch of tree far out from trunk, 5-20 metres above ground. 3-5 eggs.

Yellow-bellied Flycatcher

Empidonax flaviventris

Size Identification

Foot: Anisodactyl

Egg: Actual Size

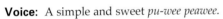
Observation Calendar
J F M A M J J A S O N D

Male: Olive green head, back, wings and tail feathers; yellowish throat and breast; wings have two yellow bands; black eye has yellow ring; feet and legs black; thin bill is dark grey on top with yellow underside or it can be all dark.

Voice: A simple and sweet *pu-wee peawee.*
Food: Flying insects.
Nest/Eggs: Deep cup built with mosses and lined with black rootlets, pine needles, grass and moss, on or near ground, at base of conifer tree. 3-4 eggs.

Nesting Location

Alder Flycatcher
Empidonax alnorum

Egg: Actual Size

Observation Calendar

J F M A M J J A S O N D

Male/Female: Dark olive/brown from head down back; wings and tail feathers black and olive green with white wing bars; throat white with a pale yellow belly; eye is black surrounded by very light yellow ring; feet and legs are charcoal.

Voice: The call is a simple *peeeep* while the song is *rreeeebeeet* or *rreeebeeaa* with the accent on the second syllable.
Food: Flying insects.
Nest/Eggs: Loose cup built with grass, moss, bark, twigs, and silky items with plant strips dangling in upright fork of tree or shrub, within 2 metres above ground. 3-4 eggs.

142

Least Flycatcher
Empidonax minimus

Foot: Anisodactyl

Observation Calendar
J F M A M J J A S O N D

Male/Female: Smallest of the flycatchers with a brown/olive head and back; rump is slightly golden; throat white and washes to a grey breast and a pale yellow belly; black eye is ringed with white; wings dark brown and black with white wing bands; tail dark olive/brown with white edges.

Egg: Actual Size

Did you know? The Least Flycatcher is not afraid of humans and in pursuit of a flying insect will dive within inches of a person.

Voice: Song is *chibic chibic chibic* repeated with accent in middle of phrase.
Food: Flying insects.
Nest/Eggs: Compact and deep cup built with bark, weeds, grasses and lined with thistle, feathers, hair and fibres, in upright fork of tree or shrub, 1-20 metres above ground. 3-6 eggs.

Nesting Location

Eastern Phoebe
Sayornis phoebe

Observation Calendar
J F M A M J J A S O N D

Male/Female: Grey-brown head and back with white throat, chest and belly; feet and legs black; white wing bands; pale yellow belly.

Did you know? One quick way to identify this bird is to watch the greyish brown tail bobbing up and down.

Voice: Song is rough sounding *fee bee fee bee*. Call is *wit*.
Food: Flying insects as well as ground insects.
Nest/Eggs: Large shelf structure built with weeds, grass, fibres and mud, covered with moss, lined with grass and hair. 3-6 eggs.

Great Crested Flycatcher

Myiarchus crinitus

Observation Calendar
J F M A M J J A S O N D

Male/Female: Olive/grey head with crest; back is olive/grey; wings are black with olive/grey edges and rust colour on outer edge; tail strong reddish-brown; throat soft grey changing to pale yellow at belly; feet and legs black.

Did you know? The Great Crested Flycatcher will sometimes use foil or cellophane in its nest because it is attracted to reflective objects.

Voice: A throaty whistle *wheeep* or a rolling *prrrreeeet*.
Food: Flying insects and a variety of ground insects.
Nest/Eggs: Bulky cup built with twig, leaves, feather, bark and cast off snakeskin, or cellophane, in natural cavity of tree, up to 18 metres above ground. 4-8 eggs.

Eastern Kingbird
Tyrannus tyrannus

Observation Calendar

J F M A M J J A S O N D

Male/Female: Black head, back, wings and tail; white chin, chest and belly; wings have white along edge and tail has white band along tip; feet and legs black.

Did you know? Size does not matter to the Eastern Kingbird: they will attack crows, ravens, hawks and owls to defend their territory.

Voice: Several different calls including *tzi tzee* as a true song. Also a *kitter kitter kitter* when threatened.
Food: Flying insects and fruit in late summer.
Nest/Eggs: Bulky cup built with weed stalks, grass and moss, in branches of tree or shrub, 3-6 metres above ground. 3-5 eggs.

Northern Shrike

Lanius excubitor

Observation Calendar

J F M A M J J A S O N D

Male/Female: Black mask that may be dull at times; long sharp hooked black bill; head and back grey; throat, chest and belly soft grey with light grey banding from chest to lower belly; feet and legs black; wings and tail black with white edges.

Did you know? This bird is more like a hawk or owl because of its diet and hunting technique. Once the Northern Shrike has caught its prey it will often hang it in a thorny bush, saving it for later.

Voice: A light song *queeedle queeedle* along with *tsurp-see tsurp-see.*
Food: Small birds and mammals but diet consists mainly of grasshoppers, locust, crickets and other large insects.
Nest/Eggs: Bulky woven cup built with sticks, twigs, grass and small roots, lined with cotton, feather and bark, in tree or shrub, up to 10 metres above ground. 4-7 eggs.

Nesting Location

Solitary Vireo

Vireo solitarius

Size Identification

Foot: Anisodactyl

Egg: Actual Size

Observation Calendar

J F M A M J J A S O N D

Male/Female: Blue-grey head and back with shades of olive along back; eye is brown with distinctive white eyebrow encircling it; bill long and black; feet and legs charcoal; throat and belly white with olive along edges of belly; tail charcoal with white edges.

Did you know? Although these birds are not common in parks, they are very tame when approached. Sometimes they will continue to sit on their nest even in the presence of humans, while other birds would probably attack or retreat from the area with a few choice tweeeeps.

Voice: The song is a series of short whistled phrases interrupted by pauses, similar to the Red-Eyed Vireo but higher pitched and sweeter.
Food: Small insects and fruit.
Nest/Eggs: Suspended basketlike cup built with bark, fibre, grass, small roots and hair in a tree, 1-6 metres above ground. 3-5 eggs.

Nesting Location

Warbling Vireo

Vireo gilvus

Size Identification

Foot: Anisodactyl

Observation Calendar

J F M A M J J A S O N D

Egg: Actual Size

Male/Female: Grey and green head, neck and back; white eyebrow extending from black bill; white chin, breast and belly with variable amounts of yellow; feet and legs black; tail and wings black with white edging.

Voice: The best way to find a Warbling Vireo is to listen. This bird sings throughout the day with a beautiful warbling sound. Song is group of slurred phrases such as *brig-a-dier brig-a-dier brigate.*

Food: Small insects including caterpillars, beetles and moths, and some berries.

Nest/Eggs: Tightly woven pensile cup built with bark, leaves, grass, feathers, plant down and spider's web, lined with stems and horsehair, suspended in tall trees at the edge of wooded area, well away from trunk. 3-5 eggs.

149

Nesting Location

Red-eyed Vireo
Vireo olivaceus

Egg: Actual Size

Observation Calendar

J F M A M J J A S O N D

Male/Female: *Spring:* red eye encircled with thin line of black set against a wide white eyebrow that runs from bill to back of head; black bill; throat and chest white; feet and legs black; back and rump are olive green; wings and tail black with edges of olive green; eye is darker brown in winter.

Voice: The Red-eyed Vireo may sound over 40 different phrases in just 60 seconds, then begin all over again. A variety of short phrases which includes *cherrrwit chereeee cissy a witt teeeooo.*
Food: Small insects, berries and fruit.
Nest/Eggs: Deep cup built with grass, paper, bark, rootlets, vine and decorated outside with spider's web and lichen, suspended in branches, .5-18 metres above ground. 2 eggs.

Gray Jay

Perisoreus canadensis

Size Identification

Foot: Anisodactyl

Egg: Actual Size

Observation Calendar

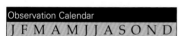

J F M A M J J A S O N D

Male/Female: White forehead with a dark grey patch on head which varies depending on geographic location; grey back, wings and tail with white underparts; feet and legs are dark grey, black bill is short and sharp; white cheeks, wings and tail are edged with white and grey.

Did you know? Its scientific name means "heap up." The Gray Jay likes to cache heaps of food at every chance it gets.

Voice: A variety of calls similar to a hawk but most recognizable call is very loud *churrrr* plus a series of whistles and cooing.

Food: Omnivorous — a variety of items including insects, berries, fruit, small mammals, reptiles, amphibians, and human food waste.

Nest/Eggs: Bulky cup built with sticks, spiderÌs web, hair and fur, lined with bark, in conifer tree or shrub near trunk, up to 10 metres above ground. 3-4 eggs.

Nesting Location

Blue Jay
Cyanocitta cristata

Size Identification

Foot: Anisodactyl

Egg: Actual Size

Backyard Feeder

Nesting Location

Observation Calendar

J F M A M J J A S O N D

Male/Female: Bright blue crested head with black band running through eye to just under crest on back of neck; black band continues along side of neck on both sides to chest; white under chin; back is blue; wings and tail are blue banded with black and tipped with white at ends; black bill is large with light feathers covering nostril area; feet and legs black.

Did you know? The Blue Jay has a bad reputation for eating eggs of other birds, and even their young.

Voice: Call is *jay jay jay*, plus many other calls including mimicking hawks.

Food: Omnivorous — in summer months the Blue Jay feasts on just about anything, including spiders, snails, salamanders, frogs, seeds and caterpillars. In winter months they supplement their diet with acorns and other nuts stored in tree cavities earlier in the year.

Nest/Eggs: Bulky nest of sticks, leaves, string and moss lined with small roots, well hidden, 1-15 metres above ground, in tree or shrub. 3-4 eggs.

American Crow

Corvus brachyrhynchos

Size Identification

Foot: Anisodactyl

Egg: Actual Size

Observation Calendar
J F M A M J J A S O N D

Male/Female: Overall shiny black with a hint of purple in direct sunlight; large broad black bill; short and slightly square tail; feet and legs black.

Did you know? Although one might think that crows are a nuisance bird, they actually devour large quantities of grasshoppers, beetles and grubs that can be destructive to crops.

Voice: A variety of calls. Most common is the long *caaaaaw* which softens at the end.

Food: Omnivorous – insects, food waste, grains, seeds and carrion.

Nest/Eggs: Large basket of twigs, sticks, vines, moss, feathers, fur and hair, on ledge in crotch of tree or shrub. 3-4 eggs.

Backyard Feeder

Nesting Location

Size Identification

Foot: Anisodactyl

Common Raven

Corvus corax

Egg: 80%

Observation Calendar

J F M A M J J A S O N D

Male/Female: Shiny, black bird overall with a blue tint; feet and legs black; black bill is long and wide and has been described as a "Roman nose"; rounded tail.

Voice: Variety of calls including buzzing, croaks and gulps.
Food: A variety of insects, carrion, small mammals and food waste.
Nest/Eggs: Large basket of twigs, sticks, vines, hair and moss, lined with animal hair, on ledge, in tree or shrub. 3-4 eggs.

Nesting Location

Horned Lark
Eremophila alpestris

Observation Calendar
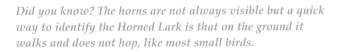

J F M A M J J A S O N D

Male/Female: Dull brown on top; chest and belly white; wings and tail brown and black; distinctive black facial marks which include small horns (feathers) on either side of its head; chin pale yellow with black band above running through eye and down; feet and legs black.

Egg: Actual Size

Did you know? The horns are not always visible but a quick way to identify the Horned Lark is that on the ground it walks and does not hop, like most small birds.

Voice: Soft twittering *tsee titi* or *zzeeet*.
Food: A variety of insects, seeds and grains.
Nest/Eggs: Hollow in ground under grass tuft, made of stems and leaves, lined with grass. 3-5 eggs.

Nesting Location

Black-capped Chickadee

Poecile atricapilla

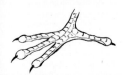

Observation Calendar

J F M A M J J A S O N D

Male/Female: Round black head with white cheeks; black chin that contrasts against bright white bib which fades into rust on belly with buff edges; wings black and grey with white edges; tail black with white edges; feet and legs black.

Did you know? In winter Black-capped Chickadees form small flocks of about 10 birds and defend their territory from intruders.

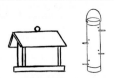

Voice: A descending whistle with two notes and sounds like *chick-a-dee-dee-dee*.
Food: Seeds, insects and berries. Drawn to thistle-seed feeders.
Nest/Eggs: Domed cup lined with wool, hair, fur, moss and insect cocoons, in cavity of tree. 5-10 eggs.

Boreal Chickadee
Poecile hudsonica

Foot: Anisodactyl

J F M A M J J A S O N D

Male/Female: Dirty brown cap with white cheeks; black chin contrasted against white belly with rust colour sides; back brown; wings and tail charcoal with white edges and black tips; feet and legs charcoal.

Did you know? During winter months they will forage for food with Black-capped Chickadees searching for hibernating insects and insect eggs.

Voice: Song is slow *chick che day day day* with calls that are distinctive chip.
Food: Insects, insect eggs, seeds.
Nest/Eggs: Domed nest lined with fur, hair, plant down, moss and feathers in cavity of tree or dug in decaying stump. 4-9 eggs.

Egg: Actual Size

Backyard Feeder

Birdhouse Nester

Nesting Location

Winter Wren

Troglodytes troglodytes

Observation Calendar

J F M A M J J A S O N D

Male/Female: One of the smallest wrens, with a very short tail; mixed browns on head and back with faint banding in black; wings and tail brown with black banding; feet and legs red; black bill is slightly white on underside; long talons.

Did you know? You may think you are seeing a mouse when you first spot the Winter Wren. They like to keep near the ground and their movements are similar to a field mouse.

Voice: Call is *chip chip* with a variety of songs including twittering and twinkles.
Food: Insects, insect eggs and spiders.
Nest/Eggs: Domed cup under roots in tangled growth near ground built with weed, twig, moss, grass and lined with hair and feather. 4-7 eggs.

Golden-crowned Kinglet

Regulus satrapa

Foot: Anisodactyl

Observation Calendar
J F M A M J J A S O N D

Male: One of the smallest woodland birds with black head stripes that set off its crown patch of orange with yellow edges; neck and back olive-grey; wings and tail black with olive along edges; feet and legs black; pale grey wingbars; pale eyebrow.

Female: Similar to male except patch on top is yellow.

Egg: Actual Size

Did you know? Their movements on a tree make them easy to spot. They flutter their wings as they look for insects.

Voice: Very high pitched dropping to a quick chatter. The song is so highly pitched that some people cannot hear its song.

Food: A variety of insects, spiders, fruits and seeds.

Nest/Eggs: Deep cup built with moss and lichen at top, lined with black rootlets and feathers suspended from conifer branch, up to 30 metres above ground. 5-11 eggs.

Nesting Location

159

Ruby-crowned Kinglet
Regulus calendula

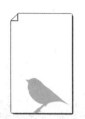

Size Identification

Foot: Anisodactyl

Egg: Actual Size

Observation Calendar
J F M A M J J A S O N D

Male: Olive-grey overall with white eye ring broken at top; crested with red patch on head; chin and neck are lighter olive-grey, feet and legs black; wings and tail black with white edges; white bands on wings.
Female: Similar to male except for no red patch on top of head.

Did you know? The ruby red top on the male is hard to see except when he is courting when it will flare up.

Voice: High pitched *tee tee tee* followed by a lower *tew tew tew* and ending with a chatter.
Food: Insects, insect eggs, spiders, fruits and seeds.
Nest/Eggs: Deep woven cup built with moss, lichen at top and lined with small black roots and feathers, suspended from conifer branch. 5-10 eggs.

Nesting Location

Eastern Bluebird

Sialia sialis

Size Identification

Foot: Anisodactyl

Observation Calendar
J F M A M J J A S O N D

Male: Bright blue upper parts; tan throat and sides; white belly; feet and legs black.

Female: Similar to male except paler and head has greyish spotting.

Voice: Song is bright whistle *cheer cheerful charmer*. Call is lower *turrweee*.

Food: Variety of insects. Visits feeders for peanut butter, berries, mealworm or raisins.

Nest/Eggs: Built in cavity of tree or birdhouse from a variety of grasses and pine needles, lined with softer material. 3-6 eggs.

Egg: Actual Size

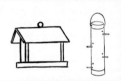

Backyard Feeder

Birdhouse Nester

Nesting Location

Veery
Catharus fuscescens

Size Identification

Foot: Anisodactyl

Egg: Actual Size

Observation Calendar
J F M A M J J A S O N D

Male/Female: Overall reddish-brown upper parts; white buff chest and belly; soft tan spotting along chin and cheeks; grey sides; feet and legs pinkish-grey.

Voice: Soft descending notes — *turreeooreooo-reeoorreeo*. Call is a loud descending *veerr*.
Food: Various insects, larvae, snails, earthworms, spiders and wild berries.
Nest/Eggs: Built of stems, twigs and mosses lined with softer material including various grasses and rootlets. 3-5 eggs.

Nesting Location

Swainson's Thrush

Catharus ustulatus

Size Identification

Foot: Anisodactyl

J F M A M J J A S O N D

Male/Female: Overall greyish brown with white belly and throat, which has dark banding; buff eye ring; pink-grey feet and legs.

Egg: Actual Size

Did you know? Very vocal bird during feeding. Swainson's Thrush is often seen with large flocks of other birds including warblers.

Voice: Series of rising whistling voice. Short call *whit* and *peeep*.
Food: Insects, fruits, spiders.
Nest/Eggs: Cup-like consisting of grasses, plant fibers and lichens 10-20 feet above ground. 3-5 eggs.

Nesting Location

Hermit Thrush

Catharus guttatus

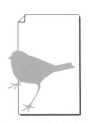

Size Identification

Foot: Anisodactyl

Egg: Actual Size

Observation Calendar

J F M A M J J A S O N D

Male/Female: Dusty brown head, neck and back that blends into a rust tail; white eye ring; wings rust when open with black ends; neck and chest white and dark spotted; underparts grey, feet and legs grey with pink; bill black and rust.

Did you know? Not surprisingly, a Hermit Thrush prefers the seclusion of deep wooded areas.

Voice: Sweet song with a variety of phrases. When disturbed it sounds a *kuk kuk kuk kuk*.
Food: A variety of insects, worms, caterpillars, snails and various fruits.
Nest/Eggs: Bulky ground nest built with twig, bark, grass and moss and lined with conifer needles, fibre and small roots in damp and cool wooded areas. 3-4 eggs.

Nesting Location

Wood Thrush

Hylocichla mustelina

Size Identification

Foot: Anisodactyl

Observation Calendar

J F M A M J J A S O N D

Male/Female: Rust coloured head fades to a brown back; wings and tail dark brown with black ends; feet and legs grey with pink; black bill has light yellow on underside; white eye ring; chin and chest white with black spotting, underparts grey.

Egg: Actual Size

Voice: Suggestive of flute, the song is a series of varied phrases *ee oh lee ee oh lay*.

Food: A variety of insects on the ground and in trees.

Nest/Eggs: Firm and compact cup built with grass, paper, moss, bark and mud, lined with small roots in tree or shrub, 2-15 metres above ground. 3-4 eggs.

Nesting Location

American Robin

Turdus migratorius

Size Identification

Foot: Anisodactyl

Egg: Actual Size

Backyard Feeder

Observation Calendar

J F M A M J J A S O N D

Male: Charcoal/brown head with distinctive white above and below eye; back and wings charcoal brown with white edges; tail dark grey; neck dark grey with thin white banding; chest and belly brick red; feet and legs black; bill yellow with black at either end.

Female: Breast is slightly paler than male's.

Voice: Song is *cheerily cheerily cheerily* in a whistle tone.

Food: Earthworms, insects and fruit.

Nest/Eggs: Deep cup built with weed stalks, cloth, string and mud, lined with grass, in evergreens and deciduous trees or shrubs. 4 eggs.

Nesting Location

Gray Catbird
Dumetella carolinensis

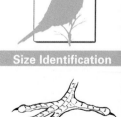

Foot: Anisodactyl

J F M A M J J A S O N D

Male/Female: Distinctive black cap with overall grey body; brick red rump which is hidden most of the time; feet and legs grey with hints of pink.

Egg: Actual Size

Did you know? Catbirds actually migrate during the night hours and research indicates they use the moon for navigating.

Voice: A distinctive cat-like song: *meeow* and *kwut.*
Food: A variety of insects, spiders and wild berries.
Nest/Eggs: Bulky deep cup built with twigs, vines, grass, paper and weeds lined with small roots, in dense thickets of tree or shrub, 1-3 metres above ground. 3-6 eggs.

Nesting Location

European Starling
Sturnus vulgaris

Size Identification

Foot: Anisodactyl

Egg: Actual Size

Backyard Feeder

Birdhouse Nester

Nesting Location

Observation Calendar

J F M A M J J A S O N D

Male/Female: *Summer*: Black iridescent bird in summer with light white speckles over entire body; bill is sharp yellow; wing and tail are edged in white and brown; feet and legs are red. *Winter*: Speckles increase and some become brown; bill is black; feet and legs are red; wings and tail have more brown.

Did you know? Sixty starlings were introduced into New York City in 1890. Since then they have spread throughout North America.

Voice: Mimics the songs of other birds and even sounds of cats and whistles.
Food: A variety of insects including worms and grubs and weed seeds.
Nest/Eggs: Loose cup in cavity filled with grass, leaves, cloth and feathers, up to 18 metres above the ground. 4-5 eggs.

Cedar Waxwing

Bombycilla cedrorum

Foot: Anisodactyl

Observation Calendar

J F M A M J J A S O N D

Male/Female: Crested brown head with black mask running from black bill, through eyes, to behind head; white outline around mask; back brown; chest and belly yellow-brown; wings black-grey with white edges; wings and tail have red tips; rump white.

Egg: Actual Size

Did you know? The name derives from the fact that their wings and tail look as though they have been dipped in red wax.

Voice: Extremely high pitched *seeee.*
Food: A variety of berries.
Nest/Eggs: Loose woven cup of grass, twigs, cotton fibre and string, lined with small roots, fine grass and down, in open wooded areas in tree or shrub, 2-6 metres above ground. 4-5 eggs.

Nesting Location

Northern Parula Warbler

Parula americana

Size Identification

Foot: Anisodactyl

Egg: Actual Size

Observation Calendar

J F M A M J J A S O N D

Male: One of the smallest warblers. Rust colour under chin turning grey at belly and rump; wings and tail feathers black with white edges; small patch of yellow-green on back; legs and feet black; black bill is long and thin; two distinct white bars on wings.

Female: Patch on back is duller and belly is light yellow.

Did you know? Parula means "little titmouse." The movements of the Parula Warbler are very similar to the chickadee and the titmouse.

Voice: Repeated song sounding like a twitter which ends in a *yip*.

Food: A variety of insects

Nest/Eggs: Cup of twigs, leaves and moss, hanging in tree branches, 2-30 metres above ground built. 3-7 eggs.

Nesting Location

Yellow Warbler

Dendroica petechia

Foot: Anisodactyl

Observation Calendar

J F M A M J J A S O N D

Male: Yellow throat and chest; olive back; wings and tail black and olive with yellow highlights; chest barred with chestnut strips; bill and feet reddish black.
Female: Similar to male only darker and lacks chestnut markings on front chest.

Egg: Actual Size

Voice: A sweet and rapid *tsee, tsee, tsee, tsee, titi-wee.*
Food: Insects with large quantities of caterpillars, beetles and moths. Young birds are fed earthworms as well.
Nest/Eggs: Cup of milkweed, hair, down and fine grasses, built in upright fork of tree or bush. 3-6 eggs.

Nesting Location

Chestnut-sided Warbler

Dendroica pensylvanica

Observation Calendar

J F M A M J J A S O N D

Male: Bright lemon-yellow crown with chestnut down sides of chest; black band running through eye from black bill; black and white banding on back with yellow tinting; wings and tail black with white edges; feet and legs black; chin and belly white.
Female: Similar to male except mask is duller and chestnut on sides is reduced.

Did you know? Audubon declared these birds as rare but, with the clearing of woodland, sightings have increased.

Voice: A territorial song—*sweet sweet sweet I so sweet.*
Food: A variety of insects including caterpillars, moths and beetles.
Nest/Eggs: Loose cup of stems, grass and plant down, lined with grass and hair, in briar tangles, hedges or shrubs, up to 2 metres above ground. 3-5 eggs.

Magnolia Warbler

Dendroica magnolia

Size Identification

Foot: Anisodactyl

Observation Calendar

J F M A M J J A S O N D

Male: Grey head with small eyebrow stripe of white above eye; black mask; yellow chin; chest and belly yellow with black banding; back grey with black banding; wings and tail grey with white edges; two white wing bars; white rump.
Female: Similar to male except banding on chest is narrower; face is grey without black mask and white eyebrow; white eye ring.

Egg: Actual Size

Voice: A short melodic song *weeta weeta weeta wee.*
Food: A variety of insects and spiders.
Nest/Eggs: Loosely built cup nest of grass, moss and weed stalks, lined with dark roots, in small conifers along the edge of wooded areas and in gardens. 3-5 eggs.

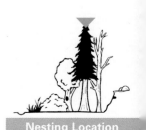

Nesting Location

Black-throated Blue Warbler
Dendroica caerulescens

Observation Calendar
J F M A M J J A S O N D

Male: Blue-grey head and back; black face mask with black bill; chest white; wings and tail black with white edges; feet and legs black.
Female: Olive-brown head, back and wings with lighter tone on chin, chest and belly; black bill; thin buff eyebrows; feet and legs black; wings and tail olive-brown with white edges.

Voice: A husky song, "I am soo lazzzzy," and a call that is flat *tip*.
Food: A variety of insects, fruits and seeds taken mainly on ground or low lying branches.
Nest/Eggs: Bulky cup of spider's web, dead wood, twigs, leaves and grass, lined with dark rootlets in tree or shrub close to ground. 3-5 eggs.

Yellow-rumped Warbler

Dendroica coronata

Foot: Anisodactyl

Observation Calendar

J F M A M J J A S O N D

Male/Female: *Spring*: Yellow rump and yellow patch on either side of chest; yellow crest set against grey head; black mask running from black bill; back grey with black banding; wings and tail black with white edges; two white wing bars; chin white; chest white with black band; feet and legs charcoal; white eyebrow. *Fall*: Similar but duller markers, no black mask, more brown and buff overall.

Did you know? A very abundant warbler that was once called Myrtle Warbler and was thought to be two different species because of its change of plumage.

Voice: Song is light musical notes. Call is *cheeeck*.
Food: A variety of insects and fruit.
Nest/Eggs: Deep cup of twigs, bark, plant down and fibres, lined with hair feather and fine grass, in tree or shrub near trunk. 3-5 eggs.

Egg: Actual Size

Nesting Location

Black-throated Green Warbler

Dendroica virens

Observation Calendar

J F M A M J J A S O N D

Male: Olive head and back; yellow around eyes and on cheeks; black throat and chest changing to speckled black on white on belly and chest; black banding along sides of belly; wings and tail are black with white edging; two white wing bars feet and legs brown-black; white rump.
Female: Yellow on throat with minimal black.

Voice: Song has a variety of accents, *zee zee zee zuu zee*, and sounds like "sleep sleep little one sleep."
Food: Variety of insects and fruit.
Nest/Eggs: Compact cup of fine bark, twigs, grass, lichens and spider's web, lined with hair, fur, feathers and small roots, in tree or shrub, 1-25 metres above ground. 3-5 eggs.

Blackburnian Warbler

Dendroica fusca

Foot: Anisodactyl

J F M A M J J A S O N D

Egg: Actual Size

Male: Bright orange-yellow chin, top of head and eyebrow set against black; black band running through eye; back black with white banding; wings and tail black with white edges; large white band on wing; feet and legs red and black; rump white.
Female: Similar to male except orange-yellow is paler; cheeks grey; belly grey.

Voice: Variable song is high-pitched and thin with a mixture of signal chirps and trills, *tsip tsip tsip titi tzeeeeee.*
Food: A variety of insects and berries.
Nest/Eggs: Cup nest built with plant down and spider's web, lined with hair, small roots and grass, in tree or shrub, 25 metres above ground. 4-5 eggs.

Nesting Location

Palm Warbler
Dendroica palmarum

Observation Calendar
J F M A M J J A S O N D

Male/Female: *Spring*: Rust crown that changes to brown on back of head and back; bright yellow eyebrow; brown cheeks; yellow chin and chest with rust speckles; yellow belly; rump yellow; wings and tail black and brown with white edges; feet and legs black; black bill. *Fall*: Overall browner and duller.

Did you know? The Palm Warbler is nicknamed the "wagtail warbler" and "yellow tip-up" because of its habit of bobbing its tail continuously while feeding.

Voice: Song is *zee zee zee* that rises. Call is sharp *suuup*.
Food: A variety of insects and weed seeds.
Nest/Eggs: Nest of dry grass and weed stalks, lined with fine grass, at the base of a tree or shrub. 3-5 eggs.

Bay-breasted Warbler

Dendroica castanea

Foot: Anisodactyl

J F M A M J J A S O N D

Male: *Spring*: Deep rust patch on top of black head; rust on chin and along sides of chest; grey back with black banding; two white wing bars; wings and tail are black with white edges; belly white with soft rust on sides; rump white; buff patch on either side of neck; feet and legs black with hints of red. *Fall:* head changes to olive/yellow; back is yellow/olive; chest is white with pink on sides, rump is buff.
Female: Duller with less rust on neck and sides.

Did you know? The quickest way to identify the Bay-breasted Warbler is to locate the buff patch on the side of the neck.

Voice: Difficult to distinguish from other warblers. Song is high pitched *seetsy seetsy seetsy*. Call *see.*
Food: A variety of tree-dwelling insects.
Nest/Eggs: Loosely woven cup nest built of twigs, dried grass and spider's web, lined with small roots, hair and fine grasses, in tree or shrub, 4-8 metres above ground. 4-7 eggs.

Egg: Actual Size

Nesting Location

Blackpoll Warbler

Dendroica striata

Size Identification

Foot: Anisodactyl

Egg: Actual Size

Observation Calendar

J F M A M J J A S O N D

Male: *Spring*: Black head with white cheeks; back grey with black banding; wings and tail black with white edges; chin white; chest white with black banding; rump white; two white wing bars; feet and legs black and red. *Fall*: Olive green overall with light banding on sides.

Female: Olive on top with thin black banding; back olive with black banding; wings and tail black with white edges, two white wing bands, chin and chest grey with small specks of black; belly grey.

Voice: High-pitched *zi zi zi zi zi* growing louder. Call is *chip*.
Food: A variety of insects.
Nest/Eggs: Bulky cup built with small twigs, grasses, weeds and moss, lined with hair, plant fibres and feathers, in conifer tree or shrub, about 2 metres above ground. 4-5 eggs.

Nesting Location

Black-and-white Warbler

Mniotilta varia

Size Identification

Foot: Anisodactyl

Observation Calendar

| J F M A M J J A S O N D |

Egg: Actual Size

Male: Black-and-white striped from crown down entire body length; feet and legs charcoal; bill is thin and black with thin yellow line at mouth opening.

Female: Similar to the male except striping on chest and belly is grey and white, throat is white.

Voice: Seven or more squeaky calls *weesee, weesee, weesee, weesee, weesee, weesee, weesee.*

Food: A variety of insects, mainly gypsy moths and tent caterpillars.

Nest/Eggs: Cup built of leaves, grass, hair and bark, at base of tree or near a boulder. 4-5 eggs.

Nesting Location

American Redstart
Setophaga ruticilla

Foot: Anisodactyl

Egg: Actual Size

Backyard Feeder

Observation Calendar
J F M A M J J A S O N D

Male: Black overall with large orange bands on wings and outer tail feathers; bright red/orange patch on side of chest; belly white; feet and legs black.

Female: Overall olive-grey with large yellow bands on wings and tail; white eye-ring, broken; yellow on sides of white chest; white belly; feet and legs black.

Voice: Song is a series of high-pitched thin notes ending downward. Call is *chip*.

Food: A variety of insects, wild berries and seeds.

Nest/Eggs: Compact woven cup built with plant down and grass, lined with weeds, hair and feathers, covered on the outside with lichens, plant down and spider's web, in woodlands and swamps. 4 eggs.

Nesting Location

Ovenbird
Seiurus aurocapillas

Foot: Anisodactyl

Egg: Actual Size

Observation Calendar
J F M A M J J A S O N D

Male/Female: Olive overall with distinctive mark on head that is orange outlined in black, running from bill to the back of the neck; chest white with black speckles; bill dark on top with yellow on underside; black eyes surrounded by white.

Voice: A progressively louder, *teecher, teecher, teecher, teecher.*
Food: Snails, slugs, worms, spiders and most other insects.
Nest/Eggs: Covered bowl, with side entry made of dead leaves, grass, moss and bark, lined with small roots, fibres and hair, on ground in depression. 3-5 eggs.

Nesting Location

Northern Waterthrush
Seiurus noveboracensis

Observation Calendar

J F M A M J J A S O N D

Male/Female: Brown head and back with distinctive yellow eyebrow running to back of head; chest pale yellow with dark pronounced banding running down to lower belly; legs pink and red; bill black and pink; short tail.

Voice: A ringing song which drops off at the end. Call is a metallic *chink.*
Food: A variety of insects and water bugs, crustaceans, small fish, mollusks.
Nest/Eggs: Cup or dome of moss, twigs, bark and leaves, lined with moss, hair and fine grass on ground in upturned roots or fallen trees. 4-5 eggs.

Mourning Warbler

Oporornis philadelphia

Male: Grey hood with olive back; yellow chest and belly with black collar; bill black with pale underparts; wings and tail dark with yellow edges; rump yellow; feet and legs brown.
Female: Hood is duller; broken white eye ring; wings and tail olive ending in black with white edges; chest pale grey.

Voice: Loud ringing *chirry chirry chirry chorry.*
Food: A variety of insects and spiders.
Nest/Eggs: Bulky cup of leaves, vines, grass, weeds and bark, lined with fine grasses, rootlets and hair, on or near ground. 3-5 eggs.

Common Yellowthroat

Geothlypis trichas

Observation Calendar
J F M A M J J A S O N D

Male: Yellow chin, chest and belly contrast with a dark black mask, which runs from bill, around eyes to lower neck; white line blends into an olive head, back, wings and tail; feet and legs grey.
Female: Light brown without the distinctive mask.

Voice: A very high—pitched song, *witchity, witchity, witchity,* that is heavily accented.
Food: Caterpillars, beetles, ants and other small insects.
Nest/Eggs: Bulky cup of grass, reeds, leaves and moss, lined with grass and hair, on or near ground, in weed stalks or low bushes. 3-5 eggs.

Wilson's Warbler

Wilsonia pusilla

Size Identification

Foot: Anisodactyl

Observation Calendar

J F M A M J J A S O N D

Male: Black patch on top of olive-green head; back olive-green; face, cheeks, chin and belly yellow; wings and tail black with white and yellow edges; feet and legs red-pink; short bill, black with red along opening.

Female: Similar to male except the amount of black patch on top varies.

Egg: Actual Size

Voice: Song is a short series of *chet chet chet.*
Food: A variety of insects including flying insects and berries.
Nest/Eggs: Concealed cup nest built of grass, leaves and some hair, on ground at base of tree. 4-6 eggs.

Nesting Location

Canada Warbler
Wilsonia canadensis

Observation Calendar

J F M A M J J A S O N D

Male: Dark greyish-blue head and back; eyes have white and yellow ring; black under eyes; yellow under chin extends to lower belly with a band of black speckles across chest similar to a necklace; wings and tail black edged in white; black bill has grey underside, white rump.
Female: Duller overall with black speckled necklace across chest being very faint.

Voice: Richly varied musical song starting with a chip.
Food: A variety of insects including beetles, mosquitoes and larvae of moths and flies.
Nest/Eggs: Bulky cup nest built of weeds, bark and leaves, lined with rootlets, plant down and hair, on or near ground in moss-covered area. 3-5 eggs.

Scarlet Tanager

Piranga olivacea

Foot: Anisodactyl

Observation Calendar
J F M A M J J A S O N D

Male: Scarlet red from head to rump with dark black wings and tail; bill is dull yellow; feet and legs black.
Female: Olive-yellow overall with black-grey wings and tail.

Egg: Actual Size

Voice: Call is a Chip burr while its song is a buzzing *querit, queer, queery, querit, queer* that is well spaced out.
Food: A variety of insects and fruit.
Nest/Eggs: Flat and flimsy cup nest on farthest branches in tree or shrub, sometimes far from the ground. 3-5 eggs.

Nesting Location

American Tree Sparrow

Spizella arborea

Size Identification

Foot: Anisodactyl

Egg: Actual Size

Observation Calendar

J F M A M J J A S O N D

Male/Female: Rust on top of head with light grey face, rust band running through eye; chin, chest and belly grey with a faint dark grey spot on chest; wings and tail brown and black with white edge; two white wing bars; short pointed bill is grey on top with yellow underside; feet and legs are red-black, rump grey.

Voice: Call is *te el wit*.

Backyard Feeder

Food: A variety of weed seeds and tree seeds.

Nest/Eggs: Cup nest, low in tree and shrub. 4 eggs.

Nesting Location

190

Chipping Sparrow

Spizella passerina

Size Identification

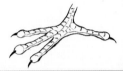

Foot: Anisodactyl

Observation Calendar
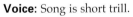
J F M A M J J A S O N D

Egg: Actual Size

Male/Female: *Summer*: Bright rust crown with grey face that has a black band running through eye; short pointed bill is black; chin white changing to grey for chest and belly; feet and legs pink with black; white eyebrow; wings and tail black with brown and white edges; back brown banding with black. *Winter*: Rust crown becomes duller turning brown with black streaks; bill is pale yellow and black; eyebrow changes to buff; underside changes to buff.

Backyard Feeder

Voice: Song is short trill.
Food: A variety of insects on the ground and occasionally snatches flying insects.
Nest/Eggs: Cup built with grass, weed stalks and small roots, lined with hair and grass, low in tree or shrub, up to 8 metres above ground. 4 eggs.

Nesting Location

Vesper Sparrow

Pooecetes gramineus

Observation Calendar
J F M A M J J A S O N D

Male/Female: Light grey overall with very fine streaks of black running down entire body; short pointed bill black on top with grey underside; feet and legs grey; back banded with black; wings and tail dark grey with white edges; white ring, and small chestnut patch near shoulder; white tail feathers are revealed in flight.

Did you know? The Vesper Sparrow earned its name from its song that may be heard in the evening — at vespers, when evening prayers were said in the monasteries.

Voice: A whistle of two beats, with the second being higher, followed by trills.
Food: A variety of insects, weed seeds and grain.
Nest/Eggs: Depression in ground with grass, stalks, and small roots, and lined with the same. 4 eggs.

Savannah Sparrow

Passerculus sandwichensis

Observation Calendar
J F M A M J J A S O N D

Male/Female: Black, brown and white central stripe on head; back brown with black banding; chin, chest and belly streaked with black and brown; wings and tail black with brown edges; tail is notched; bright yellow eyebrow; feet and legs red; short pointed bill is black and pink; white eye ring.

Voice: A faint, lisping *tsit tsit tsit tseeeee tsaaaay*.
Food: Main diet consist of weed seeds but will eat a variety of insects, spiders and snails.
Nest/Eggs: Scratched hollow in ground filled with grass, lined with finer grass, hair and small roots. 3-6 eggs.

Song Sparrow
Melospiza melodia

Observation Calendar
J F M A M J J A S O N D

Male/Female: Brown head and back streaked with black; buff-grey eyebrow extending to back of neck; brown band running through eye; chin, chest and belly are white with brown-black banding running down to lower belly; short pointed bill is black on top with yellow underside; red-brown crown with central white stripe; wings and tail brown with white edges; feet and legs pink; long rounded tail.

Did you know? Thoreau 'interpreted' this sparrow's song as "Maids! Maids! Maids! hang up your teakettle-ettle-ettle."

Voice: Call is a variety which includes *tsip* and *tchump*. Song is a variety of rich notes.
Food: A variety of insects, weed seeds and fruit.
Nest/Eggs: Cup close to ground with weeds, leaves and bark, lined with grass roots and hair, in tree or shrub, less than 4 metres from ground. 3-5 eggs.

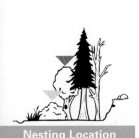

Lincoln's Sparrow

Melospiza lincolnii

Size Identification

Foot: Anisodactyl

Observation Calendar

J F M A M J J A S O N D

Male/Female: Rust on top of head with thin grey central streak; dark grey face; buff across chest and down sides of belly with fine black streaking; belly white; feet and legs pink; wing and tail feathers black with brown edges.

Voice: Wild mixture of trills and buzzing. Calls include *tsup and zeee.*

Food: A variety of weed seeds and insects.

Nest/Eggs: Flat ground in bundle of grass. Built with grass, moss and lichen, lined with fine grass. 3-6 eggs.

Egg: Actual Size

Backyard Feeder

Nesting Location

Swamp Sparrow

Melospiza georgiana

Observation Calendar

J F M A M J J A S O N D

Male/Female: *Summer*: Top of head is reddish brown and black; face grey with black streaks; black bill is small and sharp; chin and chest white-grey with rust along sides; back brown with black banding; wings and tail feathers brown with black ends and white edges; feet and legs pink; grey eyebrows. *Winter*: Similar to summer but both sides of chest turn darker brown and top of head is streaked with black and brown with grey central stripe.

Put on your hip waders to spot this bird. They spend their summers near swamps and bogs.

Voice: Song is an unbroken musical trill. Call is *chip*.
Food: A variety of insects and seeds.
Nest/Eggs: Bulky cup built with grass, lined with finer grass, in tussock of grass or in low shrub. 3-6 eggs.

White-throated Sparrow

Zonotrichia albicollis

Size Identification

Foot: Anisodactyl

Observation Calendar

J F M A M J J A S O N D

Male/Female: Top of head is black with white central stripe; white eyebrows on either side that begin with yellow tint; black band running through eye followed by grey cheeks; small white bib under chin; grey chest; white belly with faint banding; wings and tail feathers black and brown with white edges; feet pink; back brown banded with black.

Voice: Whistle is *teeet teeet tetodi tetodi teetodi*. Calls are *tseet*.
Food: A variety of insects, grain, weed seeds and fruit.
Nest/Eggs: Cup built of grass, small roots, pine needles, twigs, bark and moss, lined with small roots, hair and grass. 3-5 eggs.

Egg: Actual Size

Backyard Feeder

Nesting Location

Dark-eyed Junco

Junco hyemalis

Size Identification

Foot: Anisodactyl

Egg: Actual Size

Backyard Feeder

Observation Calendar

J F M A M J J A S O N D

Male: Dark charcoal overall with white belly; short sharp bill is pale yellow with black at end; feet and legs dark grey; tail has white outer feathers that can be seen in flight.
Female: May be slightly paler than male.

Voice: Song is a trill in short phrases. Calls are *tsip, zeeet* or *keew keew*.
Food: A variety of insects, weed seeds and wild fruit.
Nest/Eggs: Large and compact built with grass, rootlets and hair, lined with hair, concealed low to or on ground. 4-5 eggs.

Nesting Location

Snow Bunting

Plectrophenax nivalis

Foot: Anisodactyl

Male: *Summer*: White overall with black wings and tail; tail has white edges; wings have large white patches on shoulder and flight feathers; feet and legs black; black bill, short and sharp. In flight: wings white.
Female and male in *winter* have brown and rust blotches.

Did you know? Accustomed to cold and heavy snowfall, the Snow Bunting will dig a hole in the snow to escape from a storm.

Voice: Song is a chorus of whistles. Call includes *buzzy tew*.
Food: A variety of insects, tree buds and seeds.
Nest/Eggs: Cup, low to ground, in tree or shrub. 3-5 eggs.

199

Nesting Location

Northern Cardinal

Cardinalis cardinalis

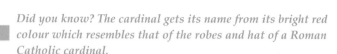

Observation Calendar

J F M A M J J A S O N D

Male: Brilliant red overall with a stout red-orange bill, crested head; black mask beginning at base of bill resembling a small bib; feet dark red.

Female: Buff and grey with hints of bright red on crest, wings and back. Stout red-orange bill with black mask beginning at base of bill (bib may appear smaller), feet are dark red.

Did you know? The cardinal gets its name from its bright red colour which resembles that of the robes and hat of a Roman Catholic cardinal.

Voice: Song is a series of repeated whistles *wheit wheit wheit, cheer cheer cheer*. Also *chip*.

Food: Seeds, fruits, grains and various insects.

Nest/Eggs: Woven cup of twigs, vines, leaves and grass, 2-3 metres above ground, in dense shrubbery. 2-5 eggs.

Rose-breasted Grosbeak

Pheucticus ludovicianus

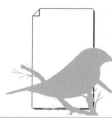

Size Identification

Foot: Anisodactyl

Observation Calendar

J F M A M J J A S O N D

Male: Large, pale yellow bill with black head; red V shape on chest; belly white with rust on either side; wings and tail black with white at edges of tail feathers visible in flight; white patches on wings; rump white; feet and legs charcoal.
Female: Buff eyebrow that extends to back of neck; brown head and back with shade of black; wings and tail brown with white edges; two white wing bars; chest and belly speckled brown; feet and legs charcoal.

Egg: Actual Size

Backyard Feeder

Did you know? The Rose-breasted Grosbeak is a fierce competitor when mating, clashing violently with other males. However, when it comes time to sitting on the nest, the males have been known to sing.

Voice: Similar to a robin but rapid notes that are continuous *cheer-e-ly cheer-e-ly.* Call is *chink chink.*
Food: A variety of insects, tree buds, fruit and wild seeds.
Nest/Eggs: Woven grass cup in fork of deciduous tree or shrub, close to the ground. 3-6 eggs.

Nesting Location

Bobolink
Dolichonyx oryzivorus

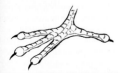

Observation Calendar

J F M A M J J A S O N D

Male: *Summer*: Black overall with pale yellow patch on back of head; back black changing to large white patch down to rump; wings have white patches and edges; feet, legs, and bill black. *In flight*: White rump is revealed. Tail has sharp pointed feathers. **Female and male** *(winter)*: brown and buff overall with black streaks over top of head; legs red.

Did you know? These birds need hayfield habitat to survive. Studies show that most young will die when farmers' fields are mown before they have a chance to fledge.

Voice: Song is a light phrase that increases in pitch and has been described as *Bob o link - bob o link spink spank spink*. Usually sings in flight. Call is metallic *clink*.
Food: A variety of insects and weed seeds
Nest/Eggs: Slight hollow in ground with bulky gathering of grass and weed stalks. Lined with fine grass in areas near water and within waterside plants. 4-7 eggs.

Red-winged Blackbird
Agelaius phoeniceus

Observation Calendar
J F M A M J J A S O N D

Male: Black overall with distinctive red shoulder patch bordered with light yellow at bottom.
Female: Brown with buff eyebrows and chin; chest and belly buff streaked with dark brown; wings and tail feathers brown with buff edges.

Did you know? Red-winged Blackbirds are prolific breeders, sometimes breeding three times in one season.

Voice: Song is *ocaaleee ocaalee*.
Food: A variety of insects and weed seeds.
Nest/Eggs: Bulky cup built of leaves, rushes, grass, rootlets, moss and milkweed fibre, lined with grass, in tall waterside plants near water. 3-4 eggs.

Eastern Meadowlark
Sturnella magna

Observation Calendar

J F M A M J J A S O N D

Male/Female: Bright yellow chin and throat separated by a V-shaped black collar; black on top of head with white cheeks; yellow and black band runs through eye; sides white with black speckles; back and wings black and brown with white edges; feet and legs grey; black bill is long and thin with grey underside.

Voice: Song is *teee yuuu teee yaar* repeated two to eight times.

Food: A variety of insects including grubs, beetles, grasshoppers and caterpillars. Also eats seeds and grain.

Nest/Eggs: Bulky cup in hollow on the ground in pastures, fields and marshes. Dome-shaped with a roof of interwoven grasses. 3-5 eggs.

Rusty Blackbird
Euphagus carolinus

Size Identification

Foot: Anisodactyl

Observation Calendar
J F M A M J J A S O N D

Egg: Actual Size

Male: Dull black overall with hints of green on head and bluish on wings; pale yellow eye; pointed black bill; short tail rounded at end; feet and legs black. *Winter*: Similar to summer but feathers edged in brown along with brown hints on head and wings.

Female: Overall light brown/grey with darker wings; slate-grey underparts; buff eyebrow; feet and legs black.

Did you know? The Rusty Blackbird will form large flocks in winter along with starlings and other blackbirds.

Voice: Song is extremely squeaky *koo-a-lee-meek, koo-a-lee eek*, with call that is *chuk* or *kick*.

Food: Insects, salamanders, snails, small fish, grains, seeds, crustaceans.

Nest/Eggs: Small cup built from grasses and moss with a mud lining mixed with fine grass materials. Builds 2 to 10 feet above ground in bush or small tree usually above water. 4-5 eggs.

Nesting Location

Common Grackle
Quiscalus quiscula

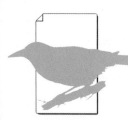

Size Identification

Foot: Anisodactyl

Egg: Actual Size

Observation Calendar

J F M A M J J A S O N D

Male: Overall iridescent black and purple; bright yellow eye; black bill long and sharp; feet and legs are charcoal grey; long tail.
Female: Similar but duller iridescent colouring, tail is shorter.

Did you know? Flocks in the thousands gather on fields and cause a lot of damage to farmers' crops.

Backyard Feeder

Voice: Chatter is a metallic and rasping *grideleeeeek*. Calls are *chak chah*.
Food: A variety of ground insects, seeds, grain, minnows, rodents and crayfish.
Nest/Eggs: Loose bulky cup built with weed stalks, twigs, grass, debris, lined with feather and grass, in conifer tree or shrubs. Will occasionally use an osprey's nest. Prefers to nest in colonies. 3-6 eggs.

Nesting Location

Brown-headed Cowbird

Molothrus ater

Observation Calendar
J F M A M J J A S O N D

Male: Brown head, glossy black overall; feet and legs black; sharp black bill.
Female: Overall grey with dark brown wings and tail; faint buff streaking on chest down to lower belly, feet and legs are black.

Did you know? Molothrus ater, the Cowbird's scientific name, means dark, greedy beggar, an apt name for a bird that leaves its eggs for other birds to hatch.

Voice: A squeaky *weee titi.*
Food: A variety of insects, weed seeds, grain and grass.
Nest/Eggs: Parasite. Builds no nest. 1 egg.

Northern Oriole
Icterus galbula

Observation Calendar
J F M A M J J A S O N D

Male: Black head; bright orange body; black wings with orange spur and white banding; tail is black with orange along edges; legs and feet grey; long sharp grey beak.
Female: Browner than male with olive-yellow on rump; orange-yellow chest and belly; head and back mix of black, orange and brown; throat blotched; tail brown-orange.

Did you know? Northern Orioles can be attracted to feeders with orange slices or sugar solutions.

Voice: Song is a note whistled 4-8 times. Call is a two-note *tee-too* and rapid chatter *ch ch ch ch*.
Food: Insects, flower nectar, fruit.
Nest/Eggs: Plant fibre that hangs from branches. 4-6 eggs.

Pine Grosbeak

Pinicola enucleator

Size Identification

Foot: Anisodactyl

Egg: Actual Size

Observation Calendar
J F M A M J J A S O N D

Male: Brilliant rose red and black that fades into grey just below chest; wings black with two white bars; tail black with hints of brown; grey chin with red highlights contrast with black stout bill; feet and legs black.
Female: Similar to male except soft grey all over except for hints of olive yellow at head and rump.

Voice: A three-note sweet musical song *twee wee tee*. Middle note is highest.
Food: A variety of insects, various fruits, seeds and flower buds.
Nest/Eggs: Bulky nest of mosses, twigs, lichens and grass, lined with hair. Low in tree or shrub. 2-5 eggs.

Backyard Feeder

Nesting Location

Purple Finch
Carpodacus purpureus

Size Identification

Foot: Anisodactyl

Egg: Actual Size

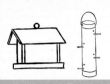

Backyard Feeder

Observation Calendar
J F M A M J J A S O N D

Male: Red upper parts with black banding on back; rump is red; chest is red with white feathers banding down to lower belly which is all white; wings and tail are black with white edges; bill is broad and yellow; feet and legs grey.
Female: Brown with white eyebrow and brown eyeline; chest white with brown streaks down front; wings and tail dull brown with white edges; feet and legs grey.

Voice: Song is long and musical ending in downward trill. Call *chirp*.
Food: A variety of insects, berries, weed seeds, and buds of trees.
Nest/Eggs: Shallow cup built with twig, grass, bark strip and small roots, lined with grass and hair, in evergreen tree or shrub, 5-60 feet above ground. 3-5 eggs.

Nesting Location

House Finch

Carpodacus mexicanus

Foot: Anisodactyl

Observation Calendar

J F M A M J J A S O N D

Egg: Actual Size

Male: Red crown, chin and chest which changes to buff at belly; wings and tail brown, feet and legs grey, grey bill, white undertail, dark brown banding around the sides.
Female: All greyish brown with faint banding down sides.

Voice: Musical warble ending with *jeeeeer*.
Food: Weed seeds, fruit, buds.
Nest/Eggs: Cup of lined weed and grass, roots, feathers, string and twigs, 1-2 metres above ground. 4-5 eggs.

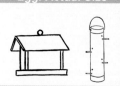

Backyard Feeder

Nesting Location

Red Crossbill

Loxia curvirostra

Size Identification

Foot: Anisodactyl

Egg: Actual Size

Backyard Feeder

Observation Calendar

J F M A M J J A S O N D

Male: Brick red overall with brightest area on rump; wings and tail dull brown with white edges; back brick red with dull grey banding; grey bill is crossed over at the end.
Female: Similar to male except grey overall with varying amounts of olive on head and back, yellow chest with slight brown banding, rump is yellow.

Did you know? Listen for the cracking of cones when searching for the Crossbill. They can be found snipping off branches with cones on them.

Voice: Call is *Chipa chipa chipa, che che che che.*
Food: Conifer seeds, variety of insects and other seeds.
Nest/Eggs: Bulky cup built with twig, rootlets, and bark, lined with feathers, grass and fur, in conifers, well away from trunk, in a thicket of needles. 3-5 eggs.

Nesting Location

212

White-winged Crossbill

Loxia leucoptera

Foot: Anisodactyl

Observation Calendar

J F M A M J J A S O N D

Male: Overall pinkish-red with long black bill that crosses over at the end; wings and tail black, with two large white bars; lower belly turns grey; feet and legs charcoal.
Female: Similar to male except greyish with olive areas on back and head, yellow on chest and rump.

Egg: Actual Size

Did you know? Their bills are used to scrap conifer seeds by forcing open the cone and pulling seeds out.

Backyard Feeder

Appear in large numbers in wooded areas near the shore.

Voice: Call to each other *peeet* with a flight call of *chif chif*.
Food: Conifer seeds, variety of insects and other seeds.
Nest/Eggs: Deep cup built with twig, small roots, weed stalks, moss, lichen, and bark, lined with grass, feather and hair, in spruce tree or shrub, 2-3 metres above ground. 2-5 eggs.

213

Nesting Location

Common Redpoll
Carduelis flammea

Observation Calendar

J F M A M J J A S O N D

Male: Red to orange cap; Brown streaking on white overall; black/brown wings with two narrow wing bars; black chin; bright rose breast and sides; brown banding on sides.
Female: Red to orange cap; brown on back of head; breast is light with brown banding down sides.

Voice: Series of trills includes *chit* during flight, *chit-chit-chit-chit*. Call is *sweeeeet*.
Food: A variety of grass, tree and weed seeds, as well as insects in summer.
Nest/Eggs: Cup shape built of small twigs and lined with softer materials including moss, plant material and animal fur. Built in dense brush low to the ground. 4-7 eggs.

Pine Siskin
Carduelis pinus

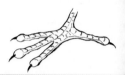

Foot: Anisodactyl

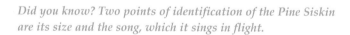
J F M A M J J A S O N D

Male/Female: Brown with buff chest and belly banded with brown; long pointed bill is grey, wings and tail dark with yellow edges; feet and legs grey.

Egg: Actual Size

Did you know? Two points of identification of the Pine Siskin are its size and the song, which it sings in flight.

Voice: Light rasping *tit i tit* and louder *cleeeip.* Similar to a Goldfinch but deeper and coarser.

Backyard Feeder

Food: Conifer seeds, weed seeds, nectar, flower buds and a variety of insects.
Nest/Eggs: Large shallow cup built with twigs, grass, moss, lichen, bark and small roots, lined with moss, hair and feathers in a conifer tree well out from trunk, 6 metres above ground. 2-6 eggs.

Nesting Location

American Goldfinch
Carduelis tristis

Size Identification

Foot: Anisodactyl

Egg: Actual Size

Backyard Feeder

Male: *Summer*: Bright yellow overall with black forehead and yellow bill; black wings with white bands; tail black with white edges; rump white; feet and legs red. *Winter*: Similar yellow is replaced by grey with hints of yellow.
Female and male *(winter)*: similar except overall grey/brown with yellow highlights.

Voice: Sing as they fly with a succession of chips and twitters, *per chic o ree per chic o ree.*
Food: A variety of insects but mostly interested in thistle and weed seeds.
Nest/Eggs: Neat cup built with fibres woven together, lined with thistle and feather down, in leafy tree or shrubs in upright branches, 1-5 metres above ground. 4-6 eggs.

Nesting Location

Evening Grosbeak

Coccothraustes vespertinus

Foot: Anisodactyl

Observation Calendar

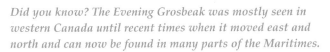
J F M A M J J A S O N D

Male: Dark brown/black head with dull yellow stripe across forehead that blends into a dull yellow at the shoulders; tail and wings are black with hints of white; chest and stomach, dull yellow; stout pale yellow bill and dark pink feet.
Female: Silver grey with light hints of dull yellow on neck and sides, tail and wings are black with white edges.

Egg: Actual Size

Did you know? The Evening Grosbeak was mostly seen in western Canada until recent times when it moved east and north and can now be found in many parts of the Maritimes.

Backyard Feeder

Voice: Call is a ringing *cleer* or *clee-ip*. When there is a flock of birds calling they sound like sleighbells.
Food: Seeds, insects various fruits and flower buds.
Nest/Eggs: Loosely woven cup of twigs and moss lined with small roots. Conifer tree or shrub, in colonies. 3-4 eggs.

Nesting Location

House Sparrow
Passer domesticus

Observation Calendar
J F M A M J J A S O N D

Male: Rich brown on head with white cheeks; wings and tail striped with black; two distinct white wing bands; rump grey; throat and chest black which turns grey at belly; bill black; feet and legs pink.
Female: Dull brown with buff chin, chest and belly; light buff coloured eyebrows and yellow/grey bill.

Did you know? In the mid-1800s, eight pairs of House Sparrows were brought to North America from Europe to help control cankerworms in crops. The first attempt failed, but this sparrow has now become one of the most common birds in cities and towns.

Voice: Repeated *chureep, chirup.*
Food: Insects, seed, grain and food waste.
Nest/Eggs: Takes over nests from other birds. Usually a large untidy ball of grass, weeds, some hair, feathers. 3-7 eggs.

Quick Reference Index

Step 1: Determine the approximate size of bird in relation to page size.
Step 2: Compare overall colour and specific markings and turn to the page number.

216 187 186 145 191

185 173 194 150 149

188 170 178 196 195

172 176 177 163 135 184

175 180 218 81

197 134 199 101 82 148

158 129 174 193 183 123

181 156 157 164 80 210

130 182 139 212 213 189

159 137 140 202 179

141 214 133

128 136 142

217 55 46 45 147

87 71 79 74 78 167

88 146 138 119

162 118 83 65

70 60 125 96 105

169 155 112 68 204 73

161 92 90 120 165 200

209 207 208 95 94 86

201 89 77 132 126

166 203 205 69 124 91

56 168 206 64

Index of Bird Names